Feminine Sensibility in THE NOVELS OF MARGARET DRABBLE

An Interpretation and Evaluation

Feminine Sensibility in THE NOVELS OF MARGARET DRABBLE

An Interpretation and Evaluation

Suhasini Tapaswi

ATLANTIC
PUBLISHERS & DISTRIBUTORS

Published by
ATLANTIC PUBLISHERS AND DISTRIBUTORS
B-2, Vishal Enclave, Opp. Rajouri Garden, New Delhi-110027
Phones : 25413460, 25429987, 25466842

Sales Office
7/22, Ansari Road, Darya Ganj, New Delhi-110002
Phones : 23273880, 23275880, 23280451
Fax : 91-11-23285873
web : www.atlanticbooks.com
e-mail : info@atlanticbooks.com

ISBN 81-269-0344-9

Printed in India at
Mehra Offset Press, Delhi

Preface

A great deal has been published in and about the subject over the past few years but the time when I started my study in 1980, it was new and at its height in India.

Actually, the subject appealed to me while I was in Gujarat. The plight of the women in the Kutch and Rajasthan area is really very bad. Looking at the pictures of the western women it was felt that the women of the West were so lucky. Lucky in the sense that they were liberated. But it was only an illusion.

Around 1980 I happened to visit Europe. During my free time I mixed and talked with women from various strata in Germany, Holland, France and England. I was shocked. Their plight was no better. It was at this time that I happened to read the literature of Margaret Drabble. It clearly portrayed the true picture of the women of the West.

Many, in the East, believed that the women of the West were liberated just because they wore trousers, cut their hair and smoked and drank like the men. But alas! it was not so. It was a very misleading picture. In fact their plight was worst than their sisters in the East.

It was then, that I took up a detailed study and found that the women of the West had to struggle for every right—right to vote, right to property, right to earn money etc. The earlier western women did not have the right to education. All sorts of theories were attached to them if they took up education.

One such theory said that biology made women unfit for education. Dr. Edward H. Clarke argued that education directly caused the uterus to atrophy. He said that factory work was less damaging to women than education because in the factory it was the body that was occupied and not the brain. In support Dr. Clarke produced cases from his own practice. One young woman, a student, had fainting spells during her menses. When she graduated she was invalid because of the constant headaches. He further concludes that her reproductive system has its development arrested because of her concentration in education. What impact such theories must have had on the women of those days who wished to have higher education is difficult to say.

This was shocking! Comparatively, ancient India has a tradition of highly educated women like Gargi and Maitreyee, etc.

Maitreyee was the wife of Yagnawalkya Rishi and niece of Gargi. Both of them had very friendly relations and Gargi loved Maitreyee like a daughter. It was she who brought up Gargi and bestowed all knowledge upon her. Gargi was so very intelligent that she could defeat the highly learned in the Court of King Janak.

Women were intellectuals and they could acquire education at par with men. Women were also warriors. In ancient India women had equal status.

Gradually things changed and a time came when women had to fight for every right. The protagonists in the novels of Margaret Drabble are from everyday life and they clearly portray the struggle of the modern women.

SUHASINI TAPASWI

Acknowledgments

I have always been encouraged by my guide Dr. R.J. Bhongle, Reader, Department of English, University of Bombay, whose invaluable suggestions helped me to develop insight into the subject. I owe him a deep sense of gratefulness.

My sincere thanks to Dr. Seema Raleraskar who helped me by sending books and articles from England; without these books the present study would not have been possible.

I must also thank Vijay Dorngade of Town Hall Library, Fort, for helping me in finding the necessary references.

Last, but not the least, I cannot forget my parents and family members who were pillars of support during the course of my study. My sincere thanks are due to them.

Finally, my sincere thanks are due to Shri G. Sastry, who typed the entire manuscript with patience and dedication.

SUHASINI TAPASWI

Abbreviations

The following abbreviations are used for the titles of the novels by Margaret Drabble. All the novels from which references are derived to build up argument in the thesis are published by Weidenfield and Nicolson of London (unless otherwise indicated). The year of publication is given after the title.

S.B.C.	—	*A Summer Bird Cage,* 1963
G.Y.	—	*The Garrick Year,* 1964
M.	—	*The Millstone,* 1965
J.G.	—	*Jerusalem the Golden,* 1967
W.	—	*The Waterfall,* 1969
N.E.	—	*The Needle's Eye,* 1972
R.G.	—	*The Realms of Gold,* 1975
I.A.	—	*The Ice Age,* 1977
M.G.	—	*The Middle Ground,* 1980
R.W.	—	*The Radiant Way,* 1987
N.C.	—	*A Natural Curiosity,* 1989

Contents

1

Woman and Society—A Retrospective View

The story of the human race begins with the female because woman carried the Original human chromosome as she does to this day. Yet for generations the historians have always regarded 'Man' as the star whereas in reality the woman was quietly getting on with the task of securing a future for humanity—for it was her labour, her skill, her biology that held the key to the destiny of the race.

The early woman was intensely occupied from dawn to dusk. Her major duty was food-gathering and this work kept the tribe alive. At no point in the history did women, with or without the children, rely on their hunting mates for food. A mass evidence also shows that the earliest families consisted of females and their children since all tribal hunting societies were centred on and organised through the mother. The young males either left or were driven out, while the females stayed close to their mothers.

Around 2300 B.C., the Chief Priest of Sumeria sung a hymn in praise of the God.[1] It was the world's first known poem but what is important is this that this first known poem to claim the attention of the world was composed by a woman. Incidentally, the first known priest was also a woman. From the beginning, as humankind emerged from the darkness of prehistory, God was a woman. However, later ages dismissed accounts of Goddess worship as 'myths' or 'cult.'

As women, they were the Goddess on earth, who held power to which man habitually deferred. A man only became king when he married the source of power; he did not held it in his rights. So in the 18th dynasty of the Egyptian monarchy the Pharash Thutmore I had to yield the throne on the death of his wife to his teenage daughter, Hatshe-put, even though he had two sons. The custom of royal blood and the right to rule descending in the female line occurs in many cultures.[2]

Woman owned and controlled money and property. In Sparta the women owned two-thirds of all the land. Arab women owned flocks which their husbands merely pastured for them. In Egypt, a man's financial independence of her husband was such that if he borrowed money from her, she could even charge him interest.

Marriage contracts, respected women's rights as individuals, and honoured them as partners. In Babylon, if a man degraded his wife, she could bring an action for legal separation from him on the grounds of cruelty. The Greek historian Diodorus records an Egyptian marriage contract in which the husband pledged his wife to be:

> I bow before your rights as wife. From this day on, I shall never oppose your claims with a single word. I recognise you before all others as my wife, though I do not have the right to say you must be mine, and only I am husband and mate. You alone have the right of departure.... I cannot oppose your wish wherever you desire to go, I give you... (here follows an index of the bridegroom's possessions).[3]

Throughout the ancient world there is also abundant evidence of women fighting as soldiers, ruling queens led their troops in the field, not as ceremonial figure-heads but as acknowledged war-leaders. Ruling woman also commanded military action at sea as the Egyptian queen Cleopatra did at the battle of Action, where her uncharacteristics failure of nerve cost her the war, the empire, her lover, Antony and her life. Warrior Queens were particularly celebrated in Celtic Britain where the great goddess herself always bore a war-like aspect. The pre-Christian chronicles contain numerous accounts of female war-leaders like Queen Medals who commanded her own forces and who making war on Queen Findmor captured fifty of the enemy queen's women warriors single handed.

At every level women made their mark. There is a record of the first known woman sea-captain in John Langdon Davie's book *A Short History of Woman.* In the fifth century B.C. a woman commanded the Athenian fleet in the Persian War in the battle of Marathon so efficiently that a great bounty was put on her head. She survived the war, but committed suicide for being rejected by the man whom she loved.

Poets, priests, queens, rulers, mothers, lovers, soldiers, captains—these were the first individual woman to take place in human history. These were the women who knew their strength and this strength was recognised because women had legal rights, access to power, education, full citizenship, the right to own money and property, the right to divorce, custody of children and financial maintenance.

No one had yet told them that women were physically weak, emotionally unstable or intellectually ill-equipped. It is only much later that the so-called advanced society made this false discovery.

As societies evolved, male took control through brutal force. One of the immediate measures was to prohibit women leaving their houses at night and during the day so as to confine them more and more to the home. Gradually, women became not only simply the property but legally part of their fathers or husbands.

Husband, home, family—for centuries the life of woman revolved round these three spheres only. In Britain, for example, women in general did not exist as 'persons' under the law. Specially, in the case of married woman the non-existence of woman was complete in all the eyes of the law. Her body, her earnings, her children belonged to the husband. She could not own any kind of personal property. Some men even argued that they could sell or at least 'lend' their wives. Of course, this was not the spirit of the law. Women were not allowed to vote. They were not given any opportunity for education. Untill the last quarter of the nineteenth century, woman's education consisted mainly of a training in feminine accomplishments provided by governess at home. There were a few schools for girls but they mainly taught the art of husband-catching to the girls by superficial accomplishments, which mainly consisted of a brief learning, of the foreign languages, singing, dancing, sewing and a preparation for flirtatious courtship.

If working-class girls went to school at all, which they mostly did not, it was to a Charity school, or part-time factory school.

Hannah Mitchell a suffragette recalled her own experience as a child in a rural area of Northern England in the 1870 in her autobiography *The Hard Way Up* (1977). The nearest school was five miles away; her father and her uncle taught all the children in the family to read, but it was the privilege of the boys to attend school, however, Hannah managed to attend school for two weeks. She was only eight years old at that time and was not allowed to go to school but felt a strong urge to learn. From the lines quoted below, we find feminism born in her from the tender age of eight. She writes that while she darned her brother's stockings:

> They read or played cards or dominoes. Sometimes the boys helped with rug making, or in cutting up wool or picking feathers, for beds and pillows, but for them this was a voluntary task, for the girls, it was compulsory, and the fact that the boys could read if they wished filled my cup of bitterness to the brim.[4]

If women wanted to achieve something, they had to be quick-witted and make most of the opportunity offered to them. Hannah did the same. She managed to turn her brothers schooling to her own advantage. She writes:

> Finding that the school master was willing to lend the boys any book they wished to bring home at weekends, I made a bargain with them. I offered to do several small tasks, such as cleaning boots, or gathering firewood, which they were expected to perform at weekends, on the undersanding that they brought me home a book each Friday; no book were forthcoming, the work would be found undone the following week, I told them.[5]

The education of Girls for the first time became compulsory in Britian in 1880, which made schooling available for all children upto the age of ten. But even then education was viewed by parents and employees as less of a necessity for girls than for the boys.

In 1837, Oberlin College opened its doors to the first woman undergraduate. This was in the United States. Its principal purpose was to provide ministers with intelligent and cultivated wives.

In 1848, Queens College was founded in London, but its main objective was to teach all branches of female knowledge and to train governesses by providing them with elementary education and certificates of proficiency.

The question of women's education in relation to men is a topic of debate even today. The theory that biology made woman unfit for education was most eloquently put in relation to higher education by Dr. Edward H. Clarke.[6] He argued that, education directly caused the uterus to atrophy. He says that factory work was less damaging to woman than education because in the factory it was the body that was occupied and not the brain. In support Dr. Clarke produced cases from his own practice. One young woman, a student, had fainting spells during her menses and when she graduated she was invalid because of the constant headaches. He further concludes that her reproductive system had its development arrested because of her concentration in education—she was also reported to be flat-chested.

What impact such theories would have had on the women of those days who wished to have higher education is difficult to say. However, a feminist, thanked Mother Carey Thomas, President of Bryn Mawa College, founded in 1889, looked back at her own trepidation in the early days of higher education for women:

> The passionate desire of the women of my generation for higher education was accompanied throughout its course by the awful doubt, felt by women themselves as well as by men, as to whether women as a sex were physically and mentally fit for it.... I was terror-struck lest I, and every other woman with me, were doomed to live as pathological invalids in a universe merciless to woman as a sex....[7]

Before Martha herself went to college she had met only one other woman who had done so and Martha's own family thought her college career as much as a disgrace "...as if I had eloped with a coachman."

Thus women's exclusion from medical college was justified not only on the biological arguments given above but also that women would be upset if they consorted with male students and with male corpses and specially if they were to be seen at work on male corpses by male students.

There was a belief among women that education perhaps might help them to escape a feminine destiny but the vision of emancipation through education has not materialised. Even today we find the woman trapped in the triangle of husband, home and family.

In spite of all the modern equipments that are available today for the modern housewife, she still remains a productive worker, because today more energies and houses are needed in home-maintenance activities like dusting, polishing, carpet cleaning, curtain washing and so forth.

J.K. Galbraith in his book *Economics and the Public Purpose* mentions such work of the house-wife and calls it "the Crypto servant functions of Consumption administration." But such language hides the chief significance of the house-wife's invisible and unpaid work from the viewpoint of the maintenance of the economy.

In the olden times or pre-literate societies housekeeping was a simple activity, because the energies of the women and also men were concentrated on the production of food. The tribes were generally nomads. They did not have permanent well-built houses. There was little or no furniture, few pots and pans and no complicated recipes to absorb a cook's time.

It is thought that 'Woman's work' is typically work that requires little training and little of mental activity. It is often described as "caring work" that is we can say, work that promotes the welfare of others rather than the welfare or development of the worker herself.

Certain work is considered good for woman because it is identified with her domestic role. For example, teaching, nursing, secretarial etc. In these jobs the woman's domestic and maternal capacities are used and so she is labelled as 'Good worker' in these fields.

Even in top-professional jobs if she was equal to her husband or better than her husband, she could not openly say so as can be seen in the case study of Cynthia Epstein, a sociologist. There was a law firm in which a husband and a wife were working together. The woman had specialized in family, land and matrimonial cases and was very competent and did the same type of work as her husband, but yet, she could define herself only as her husband's "helpmate" both in and out of the office.

Whatever may be the division of labour, a lot of discrimination is made as far as the head of a responsible position is concerned. It is commonly believed that a woman is inferior to man as an employee. A man considers it disgusting to report to a woman boss. The woman is judged unfit for supervisory, managerial or high post, not because she lacks in capacity but because it is considered wrong for men to report to a female boss.

Woman's history by contrast has only just begun to invent itself. Men gained entry to the business of recording, defining and interpreting events long time back but for woman this process has only just begun.

The movement for the woman's place in Western society began in Britain in the Victorian period and since the mid-nineteenth century, woman's progress towards equality has been more or less unbroken, an achievement that must be credited chiefly to the suffragettes as the predecessors of today's feminism.

In the late 1840's and early 1850's when woman's rights organisations began to form in Europe, woman's condition was that of a legally inferior caste. In 1865, the first woman's suffrage society was formed in Manchester and the movement spread to London, Birmingham and Bristol. In April 1868, the first public meeting on woman's suffrage was held in Britain and a resolution was passed asking for vote on the same terms as granted to men. A little later on an Act was also passed by which the British Married Women's Property Act was passed which acknowledged that husband and wife were separate individuals in the eyes of the law. Of course, it only saved the wealthy women from holding the property through trustees, it did not help in getting an equality. Neither did the vote enable women to settle down in peace because it did not give them the equality and liberty that they wanted.

So the vote was won and with it women won other rights and freedom like education, citizenship, entry to the professions and ownerships to property. But what was the chance of higher education of an unmarried mother of fourteen? She would have to spend her life in bringing up the child. What was the use of the right to vote to a middle-aged woman who is crippled with a prolapsed uterus after the birth of her seventeenth child? She could not drag herself to the polls to vote. There were many such women who were physically reduced to nothingness because of excessive childbirth. It was then, that women realised that in their struggle for rights they should first find out physical emancipation for themselves. Once they are reduced of their responsibility of child-bearing, their health condition would be better and they would be able to enjoy whatever rights they had achieved so far. So contraception became the key issue in their battle of equality.

Contraceptive preparations was not something new. For centuries women were trying to get rid of unwanted pregnancies. The methods used by them were horrible and dangerous. In Japan, Pillow-books advised a mixture of mercury, a horsefly and a leech, "the whole boiled to a pulp and taken as soon as it has come to a boil."[8]

Other countries showed an inexplicable fascination with 'animal excrement.' The first mention of contraception by the Egyptian suggests a vaginal plug made from honey and crocodile dung. In Africa, they used the dung of elephant. By A.D. 900 the 'dung' solution to childbirth had its way to Britain. The contraceptive used was made of fresh horses turd "lay it in hot gledes (coals) make it reek strongly between the thighs, that the woman may sweat much...."[9]

However hard the women tried to control childbirth, all the above techniques did not work. The machinery of reproduction was too powerful and complete to yield to anything.

The struggle of woman in the fight for contraception continued. Modern, 'birth control' as it was called, Margaret Sanger's phrase became the symbol and centre of the campaign for physical emancipation. In 1840 the first rubber condom came followed by the double syringe in 1870. The syringe had an added advantage because it could be purchased by woman as if for personal hygiene with no intention of interfering with 'nature's way.'

People who supported this campaign had a hard time. In 1877, the British campaigner Annie Besant was sentenced to prison and also lost the custody of her daughter as an 'unfit' mother. H.A. Allbutt, a British Doctor's name was struck off the professional register for writing about birth control in *The Wife's Handbook.*

In 1882, Aletta Jacobs, Holland's first doctor, opened the world's first birth control clinic. Marie Stopes headed the campaign in Britain and saw the victory in sight.

With the spread of knowledge and techniques, women were able to have control over their body. It became hard for the men to keep their women rooted in the house through multiple child-bearing.

The effects of this growing women's movement are apparent in the literature of the time. It is impossible to say when women started writing fiction. J.M.S. Tompkins in his book *The Popular Novel in England, 1770-1800* writes that most of the eighteenth century novels were written by women. Ian Watt says, "The majority of all eighteenth century novels came from the female pen."[10] However, the early women writers' relationship to their writing and to their role as a writer was not an easy one. They could not adjust to their new role as a professional writer. They were afraid that their name as a female author would draw strong criticism from specially the male readers so many of them either published anonymously or took up male pseudonyms.

Many important writers were influenced by feminist ideas. Novelists and poets created remarkable female characters such as Charlotte Bronte's *Jane Eyre*, Elizabeth Barret Browning's *Aurora Leigh* and George Eliot's *Dorothea Brooke.*

The women writers could have created greater works but they were clearly at a disadvantage in comparison to their male contemporaries. Male authors attended schools and universities and had every opportunity for higher education and extra information. Women authors on the other hand had just formal school education and no opportunity to go to the university because of their sex. It was only after 1900, university educated group of women entered the profession of writing.

The pain of not having equal opportunity as the male is clearly echoed in the novels of the women writers of the period. In George Eliot's *The Mill on the Floss,* Maggie is treated differently by her parents just because she is girl. The departure of her brother to school is a painful awakening to her inferior status. Another woman writer states:

> It is true there is little real culture among men; there are few strong thinkers and fewer honest ones; but they have still some disadvantages. If their education had been trifle better than ours. Six hours a day at Latin and Greek are better than six hours a day at worsted work and embroidery.[11]

During this time, feminism was emerging through the works of George Eliot, Bronte Sisters, Elizabeth Gaskell and the others. This period saw the beginning of a major revision in thinking about women. She was fighting for a degree of equality and personal freedom. Writings were exploding myths. Women for the first time won the right to act as guardians of their own children in case of the father's death. In 1891, the court decided: "a husband had no right to carry off his wife by force or imprison until she submitted to his wishes." Thus by the end of the 19th century, the British women were free both in person and their property and the women's movement was nearing its height.[12]

Many writers were influenced by these movements of feminism and many Victorian novels and dramas were written about the grievances of women. Probably the most effective literary creation of feminine dilemma was *A Doll's House* which was first performed in London in 1879. The example of Ibsen's Nora could not be easily ignored and that is why *A Doll's House* aroused so much indignation amongst the conservatives.

Ibsen's conclusions were similar to those which Virginia Woolf stated fifty years later in *A Room of One's Own*. Jotting down some notes for the tragedy before beginning to write *A Doll's House* Ibsen observed that there are two types of conscience, one in man and another one altogether different in woman. They do not understand each other, but in practical life a woman is judged by a man's law as though she was not a woman but a man.

By 1890 Ibsen's plays were being produced in London. They shocked the middle-class English morality. At that time George Bernard Shaw was writing *Mrs. Warren's Profession* and *Candida.* The new woman was making her appearance in popular novels such as Grant Allan's *The Woman Who Did* and H.G. Wells *Ann Veronica.*

Virginia Woolf read Well's books and agreed with the liberal and high minded sentiments which they expressed. Her attitude towards the question of women's rights was never simple and straightforward. Her energies were directed differently from the majority of feminist who were concerned mainly with eliminating specific abuses.

Her attitude was less practical than theirs but her vision was more comprehensive which can be seen in her long essay *A Room of One's Own*. Virginia Woolf's main contention in this essay is that in order to write, "a woman must have money and a room of one's own." That is she must have the same opportunities as men to pursue her interest.

Trying to answer the question "why are women so poor?" Virginia Woolf discusses the trouble they have had in earning a living. We can say that it is an essay from which the broader outlines of her feminist doctrine begin to appear.

In the 20th century, the world was helped to further emancipate the position of women because with the outbreak of the First World War, in August 1914, the women's suffrage campaign began actively to work for women's recruitment as War Workers. The London Society for Women's Suffrage in Britain promptly changed to name to Women's Service. The leader of the National Union of Women's Suffrage Society, Millicent Fawcett declared:

> A time for resolute effort and self-sacrifice on the part of every one of us to help our country.[13]

Her mother toured the country making recruiting speeches. Everyone seems to have appreciated Women's War work and the War Office, in September 1916, paid them the dubious compliment:

> They had shown themselves capable of replacing the stronger sex in practically every calling.[14]

But once the war was over, women were expected to give up their jobs and return home because as per the prevailing social thought of the time, men were the bread earners and women were home makers.

Thousands of women workers were dismissed and found no work to do. Everyone assumed that they would go quietly back to their homes and that everything would be as it had been before. But this was not possible because the war had increased the number of surplus women so that very nearly one woman in every three had to be self-supporting. Prices were nearly double and the women who had been able to live upon their small allowance could do so no longer. The Anti-sufferagate people declared that the first duty of the country was to return the women to the home. An unemployed ex-serviceman in Bristol smashed the windows of tram-cars and attacked the conductors to protest against the women's employment.

The War presented problems to the future strategy of the women's movement. However, one of the major issues taken-up by them was 'work.' It was asserted that it was work above all else that would give women equal opportunity and today, we can say that 'work' has been the twentieth century's greatest boon, to woman. Feeling somewhat uncomfortable about the way women had been forced to retreat from their war time employment, the British government conceded the right of women to became members of the House of Commons. Feminists made special effort during the 1920's to secure the election of women to parliament. A Non-party Women's Election Committee was established to help women seeking parliamentary seats. It provided assistance to 12 female candidates in the 1922 general election; only two females—Lady Astor and Margaret Winkingham won seats but several others did well.[15]

The 1930's, 1940's and 1950's were a bad time for women, had to believe that they possessed equality they found that they did not. They were seen as unequals through their biological difference from men as per the Trendian theory which was highly influential at the time.

The National Organisation of Women (NOW) was formed in 1966 and adopted a bill of Rights at its first national conference in 1967. By 1969 most major British towns had women's liberation groups and in 1970 the first major national conference was held in Ruskin College at Oxford and they formulated the following four demands:

(1) Equal pay;

(2) Equal education and opportunity;

(3) Twenty-four hour nurseries; and

(4) Free contraception and abortion on demand.

The Equal Pay Act did not originate solely from feminist pressure but the women's movements played part. Financial independence through means other than employment has been a long standing goal of the feminists and, at the same time, they have also challenged the gender assumptions of the tax system. The married men's allowance is available to men irrespective of their wives employment status. It was not until 1980's that women who were exceptionally capable were able to establish that 'they' and not 'their husbands' were heads of household and through continuous pressure from Liberals, some changes were made. In 1988, separate tax assessment have been possible made and from 1990 the married men's allowance was replaced by a married couples' allowance.

Thus, the account of the woman's history and woman's movement reveal that its impact is the same as any other social movement. Local authorities and political parties are more conscious about their impact. In parliament there are elements of a cross party feminist perspective on matters of special interest to women. This is perhaps more obvious in the European parliament.

In political parties, government departments and public bodies, women are rarely allocated safe seats or appointed to senior positions. At the European level, women's rights are salient because of the dedication of a few MPs usually female. While this is welcomed by the commission parliamentary committees that deal with 'male' issues such as monetary policies and industrial development seem unaffected.

When Margaret Thatcher became the first woman party leader and then prime minister in British history, much discussion ensued as to whether her success was good for women. For some even a symbolic victory for feminism was a victory.

Long long ago, when education was not fully developed, people relied on their ability to use physical strength. Power was important so women stayed at home and played a different role from that of today. But in the modern world, intellect has taken the place of power. There is no biological difference or any other kind of difference between the intellect of man and woman. This is proved by the No. 1 position which Margaret Thatcher held in Britain so efficiently and in India, Indira Gandhi has also proved to be an immensely capable and competitive woman.

The society in which we live today had made certain rules which are different for men and women. The woman has to perform the biological function of reproduction and, therefore, her opportunities are restricted. Moreover, it becomes solely her responsibility to take care of the children thus putting an end to all her opportunities.

The feminist strongly opposed to this practice. Betty Friedan in her book *The Feminine Mystique* (1963) encouraged women to work outside the house. She has also emphasised the damaging effect of the mother's constant presence with the child. The feminist proved that it was important to have child-care centres so that women could protect their jobs and go to work. Thus, in the twentieth century feminist protest became a major social concern.

Elaine Showalter in her book *A Literature of Their Own* describes three phases in which the self-awareness of the woman writer has translated itself into a literary form. The chronological order can be described in brief as follows:

> The first phase is the Feminine Phase which ranges approximately from 1840 to 1880. She calls this phase as a period when women wrote under male pseudonym. For example George Eliot and Marry Brunton. The male pseudonym signalled the loss of innocence and the women writers were able to write more freely. Moreover they were afraid of being noticed, commented upon and shunned from society as a woman of literary airs.

Their fear was natural because the society had so far known male writers only leaving alone a few exceptions. It took some time for women writers to adjust to their new role as a professional writer, and the readers to digest the fact that women too could write as efficiently and effectively as man. A theory which came up during this time which harassed the women writers was that only unhappy and frustrated women wrote books. G.H. Lewes in his essay *The Lady Novelists* writes:

> If the accidents of her position make her solitary and inactive or her thwarted affection shut her somewhat from that sweet domestic and maternal sphere to which her whole being spontaneously moves, she turns to literature as to another sphere.... The happy wife and busy mother are only forced into literature by some hereditary organic tendency, stranger even than the domestic.[16]

The same idea, and in almost the same words, is to be found in J. Harmilten's introduction to *Women Writers: Their Works and Ways*:

> Happy women whose hearts are satisfied and full, have little need of utterance. Their lives are rounded and complete, they require nothing but the calm recurrence of those peaceful home duties in which domestic women rightly feel that their true vocation lies.[17]

The feminine novelists responded to these attacks not by protest but by working hard to present their writing as an extension of their feminine role. The women writers of that time did not need an office or even 'a room of one's own' but they carried on their activity at home and considered it as one among the numerous household tasks. Mrs. Gaskell wrote in her dining-room and Mrs. Oliphant half complained and half boasted that she had a study but had worked in the little second drawing-room where all the (feminine) life of the house goes on whatever the problems or difficulties faced by them. Elaine Showalter points out that no sense of communality and self-awareness is apparent among the women writers of the time.

The second phase which Showalter calls the Feminist Phase ranges approximately from 1880 to 1920. The feminist writers challenged many of the restrictions on women's self-expression. Making their fiction the vehicle for a dramatization of wronged womanhood, they demanded changes in the social and political systems that would grant women privileges enjoyed by the males in society. Olive Schreiner, for example, planned her novel *From Man to Man* as a gesture of tender support for suffering sisters. There was also a highly developed sense of belonging to sisterhood of women writers. Mary Hawes in her 1984 address to the Women Writers' Dinner says:

> Our first duty as women writers is to help the cause of other women, whilst keeping up the values of the daily and monthly journals.[18]

By the end of the second phase, feminist writers like Mona Caird and Olive Schreiner were producing cogent theories of woman's relationship to work and production, class structure, marriage and family and they were beginning to work out a theory of women's literature.

The third phase is the Female Phase which extends approximately from 1920 to 1960. Showalter calls it the phase of self-discovery among the women writers. The fiction of Dorothy Richardson, Katherine Mansfield and Virginia Woolf created a very different image of woman. She was no more the self-sacrificing one. For them female sensibility took on a sacred quality and exercising it became a holy process.

Virginia Woolf's first two novels contain most of the important themes of her fiction, themes which reveal her pre-occupation with the problems of women. The heroines of *The Voyage-Out* and *Night and Day* are both afraid to marry. In each case the crucial question is whether a young woman can succeed in satisfying her emotional and intellectual needs within the framework of married life.

In *Night and Day* one of the main characters works as the unpaid secretary of a suffrage society. Having being disappointed in love, Mary Datchet decides to devote her life to the cause to become a professional feminist. Virginia Woolf contrasts the drab existence of the social reformer with Katherine's more glamorous private experiment in self-reform. Mary's suffrage society is mainly an object of satire. The total effect is interesting. Women's problems are taken seriously but the feminist societies are not. Both too much and too little is made of feminism as a theme—too much of it to remain a mere background; too little of it to become a significant part of the fictional pattern.

From the 1960's the female novel entered a new and dynamic phase which, in the words of Elaine Showalter, has been influenced by the energy of the international women's movement. Here we see a renaissance of women's writing. They have insisted upon the right to use vocabularies previously reserved for male writers only. Moreover novelists like Margaret Drabble, Dorris Lessing and A.S. Byatt have started describing female experience through artistic vision. We find in this new dynamic phase women's view of life and women's experience.

Thus the present assertion of feminism does not come suddenly but as has been illustrated, has grown through different phases, however, though today, women have equality in all the spheres of life, yet they suffer because ultimately their biology is different and it is a male dominated world.

The Women's Liberation Movement has not had the impact on English women writers that it has had in the United States and France. The media in England have been slower to publicise the movement. One or two natural spokeswomen such as Germaine Greer have been sensationalized but overall the movement is slow, but it is beginning to catch up. Parliament has passed equal rights legislation, women's studies courses have begun at major universities. A new wave of feminist energy has generated its own network of magazines, news-letters and publishing houses, designed to promote and distribute women's literature. Most of these women's presses are in the United States: the Feminist Press in New York, Daughters Inc. in Verment, Alicojames Books in Massachusetts and Shameless Hussy Press in California.

In 1975, Virago, a feminist publishing imprint in London distributed its first catalog of nine books, ranging from Angela Carter's study of *The Sadeian Woman* to *The British Women's Directory*, which tells how to get a solicitor, legal aid, a divorce, an abortion. As in the suffrage movement, a strong women's press encourages an autonomous literature. Sheila Rowbotham, one of the leaders of the Women's Liberation Movement in England, has written:

> The fortunes of the new feminism will depend on our capacity to relate to the working class and the action of working class women in transforming women's liberation according to their needs.[19]

There is a female voice that has rarely spoken for itself in the English novel—the voice of the shop girl and the charwoman, the housewife and the barmaid. These voices are beginning, only now, to emerge from silence into half-articulate speech.

With the relaxation of taboos in the open discussion of female sexual experience, and with women's increased interest in themes of menstruation, masturbation, abortion and childbirth, there has developed a critical backlash that insists that freedom for the women writers means a masculine range of experience and subject. It is said that female experience is narrow and insignificant. In the 1950's Elizabeth Hardwick was convinced that women writers could never compete on an equal basis with men because of the absolute and immutable difference in experience, she writes:

> If women's writing seems somewhat limited, I do not think it is only due to these psychological failings. Women have much less experience of life than a man, as everyone knows. But in the end are they suited to the kind of experience men have? *Ulysses* is not just a work of genius, it is Dublin pubs, gross depravity, obscenity, brawls. Stendhal as a soldier in Napoleon's army, Tolstoy on his Cossack campaigns, Dostoevsky before the firing squad, Prowst's obviously first hand knowledge of vice, Conrad and Melville as sailors, Michelangelo's tortures on the scaffolding in the sistine chapel, Ben Jonson's drinking bouts, dwelling, his ear burnt by the authorities because of a political indiscretion in a play—these horrors and the capacity to endure them are experience. Experience is something more than going to law school or having the nerve to say honestly what you think in a drawing room filled with men; it is the privilege as well to endure brutality, physical torture, unimaginable sordidness, and even the privilege to want, like Boswell, to grab a miserable tort under Westminster Bridge.... In the end it is in the matter of experience that women's disadvantage is catastrophic. It is difficult to know how this may be extraordinarily altered.[20]

But, of course, it has been extraordinarily altered. Equal rights legislation, the sexual revolution and the counter culture of the 1960's have all contributed to the change. Even in Hardwicks terms, it is now possible for women to have some of the violent male experiences she valued so highly as literary material to write, if they wish, about war and torture.

Until recently, women were the victims of the brutal male experience. But now it is being discovered how much in female experience has gone unexpressed. How few women have been able to tell the truth about the body or the mind. Margaret

Drabble, the leading British woman writer of today handles these themes in her works with artistic vision. She boldly writes about pregnancy, birth, children and maternity which reflect her to be a writer of feminine sensibility and the discussion of which follows in the forthcoming chapters.

REFERENCES

1. Kerenji, C. *The White Goddess: A Historical Grammar of Poetic Myth.* New York: Manheim, 1948.
2. Eric Nevman. *The Great Mother, An Analysis of the Archlye.* New York: Panthem Books, 1955.
3. Helem Diner. *Mother and Amazons: The First Feminine History of Culture.* New York: 1932, 15.
4. Hannah Mitchell. *The Hard Way Up.* New York: 1977, 43.
5. *Ibid.*, 43.
6. Dr. Clarke, E.H. *A Fair Chance for the Girls of Boston.* London: 1873.
7. Martha Carey Thomas. *Present Tendencies in Women's College and University Education.* London: Allen and Unwin, 1908.
8. Mandel Gabriel. *A Poem of the Pillow, The Japanese Method.* Mfribourg, 1894, 44-5.
9. Burford, E.J. *Bounds and Lodgings: A History of the London Bankside Brothers.*
10. Ian Watt. *The Rise of the Novel.* London: Chatto and Windows, 1957, 298-99.
11. Catherine Crowe. *The Story of Lily Dawson.* London, 1852, 181.
12. Lyon Blease, W. *The Emancipation of Women.* London: David Nutt, 1913, 140.
13. Marvick, A. *Women at War.* London: Fontanna, 1977, 27.
14. Rosen, A. ed. *Rise Up Women: The Militant Companion of the Women's Social and Political Union 1903—1914.* London: Routledge and Kegan Paul, 1974, 256.
15. Brian Harrison. *Women in Men's House: The Women MPs 1919—1945. Historical Jourso,* 29, 3. 1986, 625.
16. Lewes, G.H. *The Lady Novelist. Westminster Review,* R.s. II (1852) 129-41.
17. Broughton, Rhoda. *Notable Women Authors of the Day.* Glasgoud, 1983, 40.
18. Hawes, Mary. *Words to Women: Adrenes and Essage.* H.R. Hawes, ed. London: Burnet and Isbister, 1900, 70.
19. Sheila Rowbotham. *Hidden from History.* London: Pelican Books, 1973, 169.
20. Elizabeth Hardwick. *The Subjection of Women in a View of My Own.* New York: Random House, 1962, 180-81.

2

Margaret Drabble as A Writer of Feminine Sensibility

Women and their suffering is the major theme of Drabble's novels. She is strongly connected to the female tradition. We can say that a whole generation of women readers identifies with her characters who they feel represent their own problems. Her heroines are pre-occupied with the difficulties of fulfilment and self-definition in man's world, the conflicting claims of self-hood, wife-hood and mother-hood. Margaret Drabble, a contemporary novelist, is frequently interviewed, photographed and is the subject of several feature articles. She was born on 5th June 1939 in Sheffield, Yorkshire. She is the daughter of John Fredrick and Marie Bloor Drabble. Her father was a barrister but after retirement, he published a few novels which fetched him fame as a novelist. Her mother was an English teacher at The Quaker School. Margaret and her sister attended this school. In most of the novels by Margaret Drabble, the relationship between mother and daughter is treated as a main theme. The figure of the father is shadowy and unimportant as seen in *The Millstone*. Perhaps, this is because when she was a child her father was away on war and most of her childhood was spent with her mother and her older sister. Mrs. Drabble recalls in an interview she gave to *People* magazine (13th October 1980) that Maggie was a fiery child with a hyperactive mind and gave many sleepless nights to her mother.

As Margaret recalls in her biography of Bennet, her father, spoke very good English and was a charming man but her mother was rude and aggressive:

> My mother ground her teeth and everybody said 'How unattractive'—and I was in a position because of circumstances of education and money to be able to profit from her having ground her teeth twenty or thirty years ago.[1]

Obviously, drawing from her mother's life in several books, she has commented:

> I think she finds it terribly hard to read my books because there is so much that she recognizes and yet its all slightly twisted. It must be very hard for her to know that I meant and what I didn't mean.[2]

Margaret is the second child in the family of four children which includes an elder sister A.S. Byatt who is a noted novelist and critic and for a time senior lecturer in English and American Literature at University College, London.

She points out that her family was of the same size and constitution like the famous Bronte sisters of the 19th century. They were all commonly interested in writing and in their childhood composed stories together.

Margaret Drabble got married right after graduating from University in June 1960, to Clive Swift, a Cambridge graduate in English, who became a leading actor. He was a member of the Royal Shakespeare Company and so they spent the first year of their marriage at Stratford-on-Avon. At that time, Margaret Drabble was also associated with theatre and was an actress but after the first child was born, she had to give up her acting career and took up writing. The couple had three children before they separated in 1972 and divorced in 1975.

Margaret Drabble always lived with her children in comfortable house at Harristead and has always been a loving responsible mother.

It is perhaps because of this that she has been able to draw female readers empathetically to her work.

Besides her eleven novels to date, she has written several stories and screen plays, biography of Arnold Bennet and other literary subjects. She has written scores of reviews and other pieces—from short stories to extended essays—for literary journals and magazines. She writes for both school children and adults, both scholars and laymen.

She has appeared in televised literary programmes and participated in government councils, Art council committees, and British council lecture tours and for years taught adult education once a week at Morley College in South London. She has just completed an ambitious five-year project, the re-editing of the Oxford Companion to English Literature.

As discussed in the previous chapter and as Elaine Showalter has pointed out *Feminine, feminist or female,* the woman has always had to suffer and struggle. The woman's movement of course possesses a long history. Its original development goes back to Mary Wollstonecraft who wrote—*A Vindication of the Rights of Women* in 1792. Throughout the 19th century debates and discussions were carried on to consider the proper sphere of women in society. In fact, feminism was rooted in the doctrine of 'sympathy' enunciated most prominently by David Hume and Adam Smith in the 18th century. This doctrine was used by Mary Wollstonecraft in preaching feminism in early 19th century.

The doctrine of sympathy had a conscious or an unconscious effect on the writers of the century, to name a few Fanny Wright, Margaret Fuller and John Stuart Mill. We can say that their writings forecast the modern feminist ideals. Their contributions are universally acknowledged by those of the movements founders. Another name that cannot be omitted is that of William Godwin, an ardent feminist of the day who wrote *An Enquiry Concerning of Political Justice* (1793) in which he advocates the rights of women. Godwin did not merely write about feminism but actually put into practice the things he wrote while bringing up his daughters. In days when women's education was domestic, ornamental and heavily loaded with religion, Godwin taught his daughters the radical social philosophy and English history. He trained them in such a way that they were expected to be on par with men intellectually.

P.B. Shelly, the 19th century Romantic poet, too explicitly believed in feminism. Shelly's feminism becomes obvious in his comments on Plato's *Symposium*. He had full sympathy for women who were heaped by male sexism and brutality. He tried to free his sister Elizabeth from this but was disappointed because after some time Elizabeth lost her nerve and went back to the narrow pessimistic world to doom which was the destiny of most of the women.

Shelly always felt that a woman need not essentially be delicate, neat, trim and traditional. As a feminist he felt that she could do all the things that a man did intellectually. In Mary, who was Godwin's daughter, he saw all these things. She was bold in behaviour and did not have any domestic accomplishments or any interest in acquiring them. She was "never like most of the female contemporaries" explains her biographer Mwriel Spark.

It was exactly this "Womanliness" from which Shelly wanted to rescue woman. In Mary, he saw his promise and dream fulfiled. By showing the example of Mary, he proved to the world his ideas of feminism and what it was possible for woman to become. His contribution is indeed significant.

Of course, Shelly as a feminist emerges only recently—after the publication of his comments on Plato's *Symposium* in 1931. However, his poetry is full of his ardent support to woman as equal to man or at least many of his poems reveal his desire to see woman intellectually equal to man. This is strongly felt in poems like "Revolt of Islam" and "Prometheous Unbound."

In the 19th century, England was awakened intellectually. Many social issues were discussed: a major social issue being the cause of women. The 19th century also seemed to be the age of female novelist due to the emergence of great names like Jane Austen, Bronte sisters and George Eliot, and others. In the 20th century also there are a number of great women writers like Rebeca West, Virginia Woolf, Dorothy Richardson, etc., but Margaret Drabble is perhaps the most ambitious of all, she writes with broad social concern and plays a lively role in popular and literary culture. Drabble also has the strongest sense of connection to female tradition as can be seen in her novels. The novels portray sad existence of woman:

> The sexual doom of womanhood, its sad inheritance.
>
> (*W.*, 154).

Drabble won fame and reputation with the publication of her novels one after another since 1960. In all these novels the central character is a woman. She revealed in these novels, a very personal experience, personal to such an extent that in *The Waterfall* she has described with details the act of delivery of baby by Jane, the protagonist of the novel, thus showing that, becoming a mother is pleasurable but along with this pleasure there are lot of vulnerabilities attached to it.

The Victorian woman writers too perhaps wanted to write about the very personal conflicts, issues, experience and relationship but they did not have the nerve to do so. Perhaps they did not want to hurt their families or offend their friends by unconventional options. Of course, sometimes these woman novelists got around these issues by using pseudonym, e.g., 'George Eliot' was adopted by Mary Evans. But in their use of material from life, they were in bondage to the feminine codes of love and loyality. Drabble wrote these books, just about the time when sociologists and journalists were realising the problems of a housewife. So when Drabble's books were out, educated young wives and mothers were finding it difficult to adjust to domestic life. They found their own problems discussed in the novels. They identified themselves with the central woman characters and were one with her. Margaret Drabble's greatest gift lay in her sense of timing. She appeared on the literary scene as the first English woman to give voice to the delusive promise of college life, followed by the cold touch of matrimony and child-rearing.

Other elements like fate and coincidence are also to be found in the novels of Drabble, perhaps this needs illustration because she is interested in tradition. The word 'fate' has lost its metaphysical doctrine and also its conviction for the modern reader but Drabble deals with fate in a reflective manner which generate self-awareness in characters. Early novels by Drabble have characters who strive to avoid consequences of their actions, to delay or to outwit fate, even though they inevitably fail and are caught. Emma Evans in *The Garrick Year* withdraws from her conflicts, hoping to defeat them by aesthetic detachment. She sees the consequences of a potential affair with Wyndham, but she maintains an aloof critical pose, inspecting and mocking him rather than risk an embrassing human involvement. But she gets trapped in the end by Wyndham's car as she tries to duck out of sight of her husband: a symbol of fate thwarting her attempts at escape and exposing her affair.

Rosamund in *The Millstone* is Drabble's first protagonist who begins to understand and to accept her fate. The book begins with her tragic romance with George,—tragic because she cannot accept his love and has to shun him off out of her life. But the complication of her pregnancy and motherhood make Rosamund question the Providence: why was her daughter stricken with potentially fatal heart trouble? She has inherited from her parents a sincere concern for those who suffer, a sympathy that her pregnancy heightens. Her struggles have been a test of faith, and her adherence to motherhood gives her the reward of self-knowledge, at least, to some degree.

Jerusalem the Golden also structures itself around models of fate: Clara's fated meetings with Clelia and Gabriel Danham; Clara's attitude towards her home town and the telegram announcing her mother's illness, seem to be fateful signs of retribution for her neglect. Clara understands this but despite her understanding she remains rather selfishly fixed in a doomed quest for escape.

When Clara meets Clelia, the narrator tells us:

> She wondered...whether a conjunction so fateful and fruitful could have been, by some accidental offuseness on her part, avoided, she did not like to think so, she liked to think that inevitability had had her in its grip, but at the same time she uneasily knew that it had in some ways been a near thing (*J.G.*, 10).

Could she have missed this fateful conjunction? Her fateful meetings made her seize the opportunity. She overestimates her power and the significance of this meeting, and she could never escape the fate that she meets in Clelia and Gabriel because she could not see beyond the romance of the meeting and its selfish pleasure.

The telegram that informs her of her mother's cancer stuns Clara and challenges her understanding of fate. She had used her mother's illness as an excuse to leave school and go to Paris with her lover Gabriel. Her guilt seems to prove that there is a moral justice, if somewhat vindictive, in the world:

> When Clara opened the telegram and saw the news of her mother, she trembled as though she had been stuck from the heavens. She stood there, staring at the fatal yellow paper, and her first thought was, I have killed my mother. By willing her death, I have killed her. By taking her name in vain, I have killed her. She thought let them tell me no more, that we are free, we cannot draw a breath without guilt, for my freedom. And she felt in closing in upon, her relentlessly the hard and narrow clutch of retribution, those iron fingers which she had tried, so wilfully, so desperately to elude: a whole system was after her, and she the final victim, the last sacrifice, the shuddering product merely of her past (*J.G.*, 208).

Clara's thoughts, above circle round her foolish attempts to escape her fate, her mother, her ties to the past. She cannot escape her fate, yet she cannot see it in terms other than 'sacrifice.'

In *The Waterfall*, Jane Gray struggles to escape her fate but it catches her up everywhere: she can neither escape the tragic romance nor live with it in peace. Quite opposite with Rose, in *The Needle's Eye*. She enters permanent conflicts of her family on her own and makes no attempt to escape her fate. Unlike Clara, Rose accepts the consequences of these family ties in spite of the unpleasant things present there. This does not bring her happiness because most of the time she feels bitterly embroiled in a marriage she may well wish has never been. But at times we see in moments of grace that Rose is blessed with a side to her character that is simplicity and sincerity, which in some ways the opposite of self-consciousness. She stands as

Drabble's main example of the good that comes from accepting fate.

In *The Realms of Gold,* Frances Wingate has both, simplicity and sophistication but she is lesser heroine than Rose because everything comes to her easily. She is lucky and her fate brings her luck because unlike other heroines of Drabble she marries her lover in the end and has a happy family.

Drabble, in trying to reconcile character and fate, refers to the story of Oedipus and expresses her belief about fate:

> I feel that the arbitrary is significant, but it's your fate to do the things that reveal the truth to you. Or perhaps its your fate to see it later. I do believe in fate. I have had a peculiarly fated life, I sometimes think, but then if you look at it in another light, all that things happen to you and you are the kind of person that responds in a certain way.[3]

When life assumes a recognizable form, one thinks one sees the fate one has lived. But the fate may only be a way of tidying up what happens, a way of tidying up of the mess of circumstances.

Frances Wingate, as said above is lucky in her fate because in the end she can marry the man she loves. The novel ends on a happy note, but in an interview Drabble has said that an happy ending can be achieved only by a lot of tricks in the plot, and one such trick seems the use of the 'coincidences.' But there is a limit to the coincidences which provides this novel's happy ending. The narrator tells us:

> The picture post-card which Frances Wingate has written to Karel Schmidt at the beginning of the year was at that moment lifted from its resting place at the bottom of a mail bag a thousand miles away, and sent upon its way. Its journey from box to bag had taken nine months: the rest of its journey was to take a mere ten days. And to those who object to too much coincidences in fiction, perhaps one could point out that there is very little real coincidence in the post-card motif, though there are many other coincidences in this book (*R.G.*, 218).

The other coincidences are that Frances and David should meet in Africa, that Karel and David should miss a plane that crashes in the English channel, that Karel's wife should discover that she's lesbian just when Karel and Frances want to get married.

Even minor details in the novel are coincidental. In Tockley, Frances makes two phone calls—to Vicar and to Janet Bird. The Vicar is eating his supper when she calls, Janet Bird was also eating her supper when Frances calls. The Vicar had been eating Shepherd's pie, cauliflower and frozen peas. Janet Bird was also eating Shepherd's pie and frozen peas, though she had no cauliflower. There is some limit to life's coincidences. When asked about this, Drabble remarked:

> In *The Needle's Eye,* I made life as difficult as possible for the characters: In the *Realms of Gold* I made it as easy as possible. The truth probably lies half way between as far as probability goes.[4]

Drabble's earlier novels, specially *The Summer Bird Cage, The Garrick Year* and *The Millstone* are in the first-person narration and since all the three are in the first-person, it is hard to know when the protagonists are self-portraits of Margaret Drabble and when they are simply intended to represent members of her own age group. When she was asked whether she was working out her own problems in her first three novels, Drabble answered:

> It's almost inevitable, I think, that one should write about ones age group and the preoccupations of it.[5]

But Sarah, Emma and Rosamund seem to be more than fictional members because they represent their creator in certain very detailed ways. Sarah and Rosamund are Oxford English majors like Drabble and like her they have important and complex relationship with their sisters. For example, in *The Millstone* when Rosamund becomes pregnant she writes about it to her sister Beatrice. Beatrice's response is worth quoting:

> I must say you didn't go into many details about the whole thing, but from what you said I gathered you were intending to keep the child. I feel I must tell you that I

> think this is the most dreadful mistake and would be frightful for both you and the child—just think, if you had it adopted, you could forget about the whole business in six months and carry on exactly where you left off.... I just can't see you adapting yourself to the demands it would make on you, you have always been so set on your independence and having your own way.... However, it isn't just you that I am thinking of. It would be bad enough for you but it would be far, far worse for the child. Through no fault of its own it would have to have the shun of illegitimacy all its life and I can't tell you how odiously cruel and vicious children can be to each other, once they get hold of something like that. A baby isn't something you can have just because you feel you ought to (*M.*, 66-67).

This letter says some good things about Beatrice. First, she knows her sister well and that there would be a conflict in Rosamund's life in raising the child and her own independence because throughout the novel Rosamund's independent nature has been stressed. Secondly, the letter also shows that Beatrice truly loves her sister and does not want her to suffer because of wrong decision. Besides, she also thinks about the child and its welfare.

Rosamund's response to the letter is one of full of anger because she feels nobody has the faintest right to advise about her child. She remarks:

> Nobody had the faintest right to offer me any advice about my own child...her letter revealed to me the depth of my determination to keep the baby. The determination at this stage cannot have been based, as it later was, on love, for I felt no love and little hope of feeling it; it was based rather on an extraordinary confidence in myself, in a conviction, quite irrational, that no adoptive parents could ever be as excellent as I myself would be (*M.*, 67-68).

The above response of Rosamund to Beatrice's letter is rather crude. Beatrice is full of concern for her sister but Rosamund's response to it is full of anger, showing the complex relationship between the sisters.

Further autobiographical evidences are to be found in Drabble's other works. *The Garrick Year* is clearly based on a year Drabble and her husband spent in Stratford-on-Avon and it is an open secret that the novel arose out of Drabble's boredom and resentment when she followed her husband to the Royal Shakespeare Theatre at Stratford-on-Avon. In *The Needle's Eye* the heroine Rose goes back to her husband at the end of the novel. Actually this is not good for her but Drabble ends the novel with this moral tone and she has admitted that Rose's return to Christopher paralleled her own inability to break with her husband at the time she was writing the novel.[6]

Jerusalem the Golden is even more candidly autobiographical. In her biography of Bennet, Drabble says she based the novel on her childhood memories of Sheffield: "I wrote the book from memory."[7] Like Drabble, the heroine of *Jerusalem the Golden* grows up in the barren territory of the industrial north of England. Her mother is both dour and self righteous or as Drabble has said of her own mother, "depressed and depressing." (Hardin, Interview) Clara views winning a scholarship to London University (as Drabble may have anticipated going to Cambridge) as her chance to escape to "some less obstinately alien world" (*J.G.* 73). In her final year at the university she finds that and more, "a truly terrestrial paradise, where beautiful people in beautiful houses spoke of beautiful things" (*J.G.* 37). Clara meets in short, the Denhams, a large colourful, affectionate family, the antithesis of her own. In her interview with Drabble, Nancy Hardin observed:

> A significant characteristic of the young women in your novels is their inability to accept the values of their parents. Instead they commit themselves to a search for 'chosen' or 'extended' families with whom they work through their identities and beliefs. Clara Mangham of *Jerusalem the Golden* come to mind.

Drabble's response is revealing:

> I have often wondered whether this is a problem that is particular to me in any way, or whether it's a problem that

> afflicts almost all girls, and men too—that one has to escape from one's own family and find substitute families or substitute patterns of living, I don't know whether this might reveal my own feeling about my own family background. For many years my mother was very depressed. She's now not, thanks, to well quite frankly, thanks to drugs. So throughout my adolescence I was struggling with the fact that adult life seemed to be incredibly depressing...one had to find some image of liveliness or colour or love that was different from what one had been brought upon. I don't know how I would have developed if I'd known my mother as she is now. She is so much more cheerful and active. I might have had a completely different view of needing to leave the family or having to find other mother figures. But I certainly do—did, I think—look for other mother figures...what one is looking for is just patterns of living in other people.[8]

As Drabble has said in her interview, Clara too finds patterns of living in the Denham house but unlike Drabble and her husband, Clara and her lover do not separate at the end of the novel.

Further striking parallels are found between Kate Armstrong, the heroine of *The Middle Ground* and Margaret Drabble. Both of them have generated their early works out of their identity as women and both of them were viewed as writers of women's work and champions of feminist perspectives. Kate Armstrong in the novel is tired of dealing with women. At one point she remarks:

> I am bloody sick of bloody women.... I am sick to death of them, I wish I'd never invented them, but they won't just go away because I am tired of them. Will they? (*M.G.*, 8)

Margaret Drabble too, initially wrote enthusiastically about women and their problems but was later, tired of being labelled as a women's writer and so from *The Ice Age* onwards turned increasingly to the social scene from the individual psyche.

These autobiographical elements are found in Drabble's work because she wrote from real experience, particularly women's experience and it is here that her feminine sensibility is evident. She has commented that she was profoundly affected by reading Simone de Beauvoir's *The Second Sex* while she was at Cambridge, she remarks:

> This seemed to me to be wonderful material and so important to me as a person. It was material that nobody had used, and I could use, as nobody had ever used as far as I would use it.[9]

The second sex is an anatomy of what Drabble has called 'the situation of being a woman' in a man's world. It asserts that one is not born but becomes a woman. de Beauvoir describes "how woman undergoes her apprenticeship, how she experiences her situation, in what kind of universe she is confined, what modes of escape are vouchsafed her."[10]

The crucial discovery a woman makes during her apprenticeship to life is that she is confined to a sphere created and ordained for her by men, and Drabble's early novels resound with this discovery. As she told one interviewer:

> in my earlier novels, I wrote about the situation of being a woman—being stuck with a baby, or having an illegitimate baby, or being stuck with a marriage where you couldn't have a job.[11]

But what a woman is really stuck with in our culture is the condition de Beauvoir describes as 'alterity' which means that she is defined in relation to man. "Now what peculiarly signalizes the situation of woman is that she—a free and autonomous being like all human creatures—nevertheless finds herself living in a world where men compel her to assume the status of the other" (*T.S.S.*, 28). In patriarchy, "humanity is male and man defines woman not in herself but as relative to him.... He is the subject, he is the Absolute—she is the other." Specifically, de Beauvoir says, man has decreed that woman is, "the sex, by which is meant that she appears essentially to the male, as sexual being" (*T.S.S.*, 16). Men, "propose to stabilise her as sexual object and to doom her to immanence" (*T.S.S.*, 28). Can a woman in this situation, de Beauvoir asks, become "an autonomous and transcendent subject?" (*T.S.S.*, 278). Without employing, perhaps, without even fully understanding de Beauvoir's existentialist vocabulary, Margaret Drabble seems in her early novels to be exploring some of the practical implication of *The Second Sex.*

There is a deeply personal, honest and exploratory quality about Margaret Drabble's work. Her works are moral and humanistic in nature. Her strength as a writer is in the way she has tuned herself to her time and her concern with social determinism and historical change has in some ways made her more of a realist with an acute feminine sensibility.

Taken as a whole, her work shows new morality against the old, incorporating the viewpoint of the intellectual socialist wife and mother. She is sometimes dismissed as a 'Hamstead novelist' because her characters live in or around that fashionable and expensive area of London, inhabited by rich socialists and famous writers like herself. Drabble's novels draw the reader to the tension exemplified by Drabble and experienced by many contemporary women who are struggling to define themselves within a patriarchal frame of reference. The strength of these characterizations stems from her own unresolved questioning and her experience of living in what she has termed as the 'unchartered world' of modern female identity:

> We do not want to resemble the woman of the past, but where is our future? This is precisely the question that many novels written by women are trying to answer: some in comic terms, some in tragic, some in speculative. We live in an unchartered world, as far as manners and morals are concerned, we are having to make up our morality as we go. Our subject matter is enormous, there are whole new patterns to create.[12]

REFERENCES

1. Iris Rozenewajof. Interview with Margaret Drabble. *Women's Studies,* 6 (1979) 339.
2. *Ibid.,* 335.
3. Dee Preussner. Talking with Margaret Drabble. *Modern Fiction Studies,* 20, 4 (1979-1980) 567.

4. Monica Laurifzen Mannheimer. *The Search for Identity in Margaret Drabble's The Needle's Eye. Dutch Quarterly Review of Anglo American Letters,* Vol. No. 1 (1975) 38.
5. Peter Firchow. *Margaret Drabble in the Writer's Place*: Interview on the Literary Situation in Contemporary Britain. Minneapolis: University of Minnesota Press, 1974, 102-121.
6. Nancy S. Hardin. An Interview with Margaret Drabble. *Contemporary Literature,* 14 (Summer 1973) 227.
7. Margaret Drabble. *Arnold Bennet.* New York: Alfred K. Knopf, 1974, 5.
8. Nancy S. Hardin. An Interview with Margaret Drabble. *Contemporary Literature,* 14, 3 (Summer 1973) 273-295.
9. Peter Firchow. *Margaret Drabble in the Writer's Place*: Interview on the Literary Situation in Contemporary Britain. Minneapolis: University of Minnesota Press, 1974, 107.
10. Simon de Beauvoir. *The Second Sex,* Trans. H.M. Parsuley. New York: Alfred A. Knopt, 1953, 24.
11. Interview with Nancy Poland. *Margaret Drabble: There Must be a Lot of People Like Me. Midwest Quarterly,* XVI, 3 (1975) 267.
12. Margaret Drabble. *A Woman Writer. Book,* 11 (1973) 6.

3

Analysis of the Major Novels of Margaret Drabble

Margaret Drabble's novels to date run from *A Summer Bird Cage* (1963) to *The Middle Ground* (1980). Her novels, we can say, are highly literary because many of them have literary or religious quotations and there are references to other writers, particularly *A Summer Bird Cage* reminds us of Jane Austen's *Pride and Prejudice* and *The Waterfall* reminds us of *The Mill on the Floss* by George Eliot.

All her novels have a typical feminine insight and with the exception of *The Ice Age* all her novels are closely linked to the woman's experience. She is, therefore, regarded as a "Women's novelist." If a women's novelist is someone whose subject is women, then the author of *A Summer Bird Cage, The Garrick Year* and *The Millstone* was a women's novelist. In these novels her subject was, what it was like to be a woman in a world which calls woman the second sex. As said in the earlier chapter, she was profoundly influenced by Simon de Beauvoir's *The Second Sex*.

In her first novel, *A Summer Bird Cage,* Drabble uses bird cage as an image of a trap in which a woman often finds herself. It is a story of Sarah Bennett, a young woman blessed with intelligence and good looks but she does not know what she should do as a woman. At a cocktail party someone asks her, "And what will you be?" "How should I know?" Sarah replies, "I will be what I become, I suppose" (*S.B.C.*, 7).

Though Sarah answers in a non-chalant manner, this non-chalance is superficial because it was this very question which kept her worried year in and year out.

The novel was written in 1963. At that time many women had graduated from Oxford and other Universities. These women who were Over-educated found that they lacked a sense of vocation, they did not want to get married and be restricted to the house, the kitchen, the children and the embroidery. The story of Sarah is the same. She feels depressed over the shapelessness of woman's life and thus expresses miserably:

> Men are alright, they are defined and enclosed but we in order to live must be open and raw to all comers. What happens otherwise is worse than what happens normally the embroidery and the children and the sagging mind. I felt doomed to defeat. I felt all women were doomed (*S.B.C.*, 28-9).

Unable to commit herself to marriage, Sarah takes up a job at the BBC and shares a flat with a college friend whose name is Gill. Gill has separated from her husband and in her, Sarah sees the folly of blindly leaping into marriage of love. Lousie is Sarah's sister who is married and who has tried to force marriage into a new mould by marrying money and choosing adultery. So far, there had been examples of men marrying rich women and committing adultery but Drabble has reversed the pattern. Here Lousie marries a rich man and commits adultery.

Sarah is fascinated with the details of Lousie's private life, her dirty underwear (*S.B.C.*, 28), the interior of her closet (*S.B.C.*, 140) and above all her bedroom. Invited to a party at Lousie's place, Sarah takes the advantage of the suggestion that she leave her coat in the bedroom. Sarah takes this opportunity to look around. Her gaze moves from the "white plaster frieze and cupids on the ceiling" to Lousie's dressing table and cosmetics, and finally to 'the big double bed.' She remarks:

> Suddenly I felt rather guilty and inquisitive, sitting in their bedroom and speculating on what they looked like in bed, as if I had been reading a diary instead of simply receiving unrejectable impressions...(*S.B.C.*, 129).

Sarah is shocked when she comes to know that Lousie has been sleeping not with her husband but with her lover. Drabble has compared this state of mind of Sarah with that of children who find out about sex for the first time. The children, too, initially are shocked, surprised and yet oddly certain that it must be so. Sarah's state becomes like the children and she becomes obsessed with sex but at the same time she is terrified.

However, one day, Stephan, Lousie's husband, catches Lousie with her lover in the bath-tub and throws her out of the house. John, Lousie's lover, who is literally waiting in the wings takes her with him. Now this sort of coincidence that as soon as one man throws her out, the other is waiting is too much of an exaggeration and looks too common place.

Sarah had always looked upto Lousie's marriage as a model. But this model is broken. Then, she had always looked up to Daphne, her cousin, as an ideal female. But Sarah's description of Daphne is rather bitchy. She portrays her as a stereotypical old maid. Sarah reflects:

> I have nice legs, whereas Daphne's are muscular and shapeless round the ankles and covered in hairs and bluish pimples. Oh, the agony. If I had any coverage I would have told her to put on suntan stockings, but somehow I couldn't interfere with the awfulness of nature. It must be so frightful to have to put things on in order to look better, instead of to strip things off (*S.B.C.*, 119).

Sarah, after this speculation, acknowledges that she's being a bitch. The original Daphne she remembers was chased by God and was turned into a tree to preserve her virginity. Sarah feels that her cousin Daphne was like the original Daphne and had succeeded in preserving her virginity.

Whatever may be the description of Daphne, Sarah finds her sexless and Sarah is afraid of being like her. She does not want to be 'unsexy' like Daphne but she cannot be sexless like Simene because, Sarah, many a time has strong desires for sex and even has fantasies of her gown slipping down her shoulder but when it comes to 'experiencing' sex, she draws back. Drabble has dramatised in Sarah a typical situation a young girl faces when she has grown up into an adult.

While reading the novel, *A Summer Bird Cage*, we are reminded of Jane Austen's *Pride and Prejudice* because after all *A Summer Bird Cage* draws neatly wrought comparisons and contrasts of marriage types.

It is not merely a matter of marrying well but of charting ones own identity in a changing social world. However, the options for the modern Bennetts are much more extensive.

The novel takes an interesting turn only when Sarah starts speaking honestly and thoughtfully about the female identity. She would like to be an 'high powered woman' and is flattered when one of the male acquaintances calls her so.

The novel is in the first-person narration and Sarah narrates that her fiancee named Francis was in America. They were in Oxford for a year and fell in love. He was awarded a commonwealth scholarship to study political theory at Harward. However while reading the novel, one thing that pinches the mind is the contradiction in Sarah's narration. In the beginning she says that it is a sheer stupidity to believe that a woman was nothing without a man but towards the end of the novel she confesses that her life has been in a limbo-like state during the absence of Francis. She would resume her normal gay life after his return. Thus, she supports the very statement to which she had objected earlier. In the beginning she says, "the days are over, thank God, when a woman justifies her existence by marrying." But towards the end she seems to return back to the traditional role of a woman, waiting for Francis and not feeling the life same without him.

In *A Summer Bird Cage,* Drabble has been able to show clearly how uncertain a woman feels once she is out of the university. She does not know what to do with her life. The events that occur in Sarah's life are trivial but it is true that a woman's life at this stage is trivial. Marriage vs. Career. Sarah is exploring both the possibilities. None of the marriages she sees is encouraging. One is happy but dull, another exhilarating but self-destructive, and a third her sister Lousie's, in which she had hoped to find a model of her own, ends in a divorce. She seems to have a natural bent for scholarship. Asked by her sister's lover what she would most like to achieve in her life, she says that she would like to write a book (*S.B.C.*, 196). And one of her reasons for despising Lousie's novelist husband is that he talks about novels "so professionally, whereas these things were life and death to me" (*S.B.C.*, 63).

Sarah is standing on that path of life where she does not know what to do. For Virginia K. Beards "Sarah's story illustrates the secondary status of the educated woman within the patriarchy."[1]

It may be right in a way but the primary focus of *A Summer Bird Cage* is not the status within patriarchy of an educated young woman like Sarah, but her psychology, and Drabble has been highly successful in portraying this.

Drabble's second novel, *The Garrick Year* (1964), came soon after *A Summer Bird Cage*. The story revolves round Emma, the protagonist of the novel. In *A Summer Bird Cage*, Lousie Bennett's marriage is shown through the eyes of Sarah as "an enterprise worth consideration." In *The Garrick Year*, the 'anatomy' of that marriage is seen.

Twenty-six years old Emma is married to David, the actor. They have two children. Emma has to give up her chance of a career as television news reader in order to stay with her husband in Herford. Emma spends a grudging life at Herford where she is transferred because while her husband is away at the theatre she is rooted to the house with the children. She then decides to take a lover and her choice is David's producer and director, Wyndham Farrah, who responds quickly to her flirtation and initiates a series of weekly clandestine meetings. Emma, here reminds one of Louise. Emma, like Louise dines out often. Yet she doesn't seem to take pleasure in the lovely meals. Sarah, however, eats and drinks heartily, Emma only nibbles. She takes pleasure neither in eating or seeing others eat. When she is not dinning out, Emma is shown spending a great deal of her time preparing and serving meals for others.

There are two other women characters. One is Mary Scott, Emma's school friend and the other Sophy Brent, the actress working with her husband. Mary Scott exemplifies middle-class values in which Emma has been brought up. Generally, the middle-class values are good taste, intelligence and respectability. Sophy Brent, on the other hand, is just the opposite of Mary Scott. She is shallow, self-centred, vulgar and loose in morals. She has an affair with Mary's husband. Emma is disgusted when Sophy comes to tea and eats everything within sight, spreading far more jam on her bread than it is decent in company and dropping crumbs of bread all over. Between the two, Emma tries to find a pattern for self and admits that she would rather be like Sophy for she says, "my tastes are shallow, my life is shallow and I like anonymity, change and fame" (*G.Y.*, 100).

It is perhaps because of this outlook of life, she feels she would do something different from the other housewives—something beyond the traditional role. That is why, perhaps, she has an affair with Wyndham Farrah. But Drabble's characters are rooted within a particular mind and body. They belong to that social class where morality is important. Emma from the beginning maintains a strict self-control. At onc point Farrah remarks:

> Trying to get a kiss out of you is like trying to get blood out of a stone (*G.Y.*, 140).

Emma's affair with Farrah is a challenge to her domestic self because as she herself says, she did not want an easy life but wanted something precipitous. Yet, Emma prevents everything that is precipitous in her marriage. Her marriage is characterised by her oppressive self-sacrificing domesticity and her compulsive orderliness which she recognizes as defences against the very chaos she claims to desire. Similarly, she characterises her infrequent sexual encounters with David as 'legalized rape.' This we can say, happens because of Emma's inability to respond to the nature, either inside or outside herself.

We see this in the scene when she and Wyndham go to look at his aunt's house, and she is totally unnerved by the landscape, a reality outside the narrow human control within which she has tried to live. During this visit she stumbles over an apple that is rotton. The apple symbolizes that temptations decay before she can bring herself to taste the forbidden fruit.

The sexual life of Emma becomes a sad comedy because she tells David that the children and their sexual encounters are only legalised rape. She has a lover, but with him too she cannot enjoy sex and she desperately remarks after her encounter with Wyndham, "I wish to God that I could say that I enjoyed it" (*G.Y.*, 61).

During her affair with Farrah, Emma meets with a number of accidents which fill her mind with doubts about her relationship with Farrah. For instance, one evening when she is out with Farrah the gas is left on and her household is threatened. On another occasion, she is accidentally pinned against the garage wall by Farrah's car as her husband comes home and lastly, the near drowning of her daughter into the river Rye. All these incidents made her realise that the affair was not proper. Moreover, she never enjoyed it. Drabble has effectively brought out the dilemma between Emma and which is suggestive. She lives a sheltered life behind a cultivated social front and so is unable to undertake any significant action. In fact, Emma is glad when the affair is over.

The first person narration of Emma is very complex because the book is full of contradictions. For example, Emma tells us that she has an affair with Farrah because the ideal enchants her. Sexually she is unresponsive because she associates Love-making with having babies. That is why she could not enjoy sex. But while saying all this she immediately makes a contradiction and says that children are such a great joy. Her contradictions about herself not only meddle her life but perplex the readers so that one agrees when Dee Preussner says:

> Emma has no essential self, but remains an accumulation of roles.[2]

In the end, Emma learns to accommodate herself in her various roles as wife, mother and lover—putting an end to her self-hood. She succeeds in forcing marriage into a mould which both she and her husband find sufficiently comfortable. They are brought close to each other by their daughter who falls into the river Rye, and is about to be drowned. This real event assumes symbolic meaning when Emma remembers a song:

> Mother may I go out to swim,
> O yes, my darling daughter,
> O yes, you may go out to swim,
> But don't go near the water (*GY.*, 198).

Symbolically, "Don't go near the water" means "don't get wet with milk and blood and tears a varied sea of grief" (*GY.*, 190). Margaret Drabble, a novelist of feminine sensibility, wants to indicate that the wetness is the essence of female sexuality — the blood of menstruation, the lubricity of the ready vagina, the broken sac of amniotic fluid.

On the symbolic level to be drawn means to yield, to ascent to, ones own sexuality. Julian, an homosexual actor working with David is unable to resist the attraction of another male actor and so ultimately goes to the river Rye and is drowned. His drowning, according to Emma represents his acceptance of his homosexuality. But Emma will not accept her sexuality she says:

> You will not find me at the bottom of any river. I have grown into the earth, I am terrestrial (*GY.*, 219).

The novel ends with Emma remaining married. The character of Emma has been sketched very intelligentiy by Drabble because though she is the heroine and the central figure of the novel, she commits adultery. But it is a very strange adultery, consisting of endless dinners out and rides in cars and caresses restricted to above the waist. Emma declares a passion for her lover but it is more like a school girl crush, the affair is consummated only once, briefly, when she is in bed with cold, and she does not enjoy it. Emma does not seem to like sex at all; she describes herself as 'frigid' and tells her husband the children were the result of legalised rape. Her husband seems even more selfish than she is, for he not only accuses her of being out of date but also has Sophy as his mistress. However, Emma has chosen him with the perversity which is an admitted aspect of her character. She is excited by domination and threat, though she sulks at the practical effects. She strikes martyred attitude.

She has imagined married life would be a nightmare, an adventure...whatever else...exciting.

Emma is attracted by David's flashy commercial, drunken, photogenic selfishness and he by her cool, professional aesthetic privileged photogenic eccentricity. Emma is beautiful in a bony, stick-like, dun-coloured way and has appeared on the covers of glossy magazines. It is hardly surprising that so many women try to identify with Drabble women, who are always good looking, always intelligent and usually at some point of female crisis.

It is an open secret that the novel arose out of Drabble's boredom and resentment when she followed her husband to the Royal Shakespeare Theatre at Stratford-on-Avon, where he played good parts, while she understudied, but the stars remained, in her own words 'disgustingly healthy.' But Emma is not the serious, intellectual Drabble; or if she is, Emma represents rebellion against circumstances by means of exploring after ego, irresponsible, selfish and immature, like the child's imaginary companion who does all the 'naughty' things the child cannot admit to. Drabble herself says the novel probably contained much 'undigested unhappiness.'

When Valerie Myer interviewed her in 1970 for the *Times Educational Supplement*, she told Drabble that she found the character of Emma as a satirical portrait of a silly woman, but Drabble retorted, by telling that "She is not silly."

This shows, Drabble has respect for her character and sympathy for Emma's plight, which was in many respects her own.

In a scene in the novel, Emma is shown fishing, boiling hot nappies out of the washing machine with a pair of wooden tongs. Until about 1980, disposable nappies were unknown and towelling nappies were rinsed and washed. Emma has a washing machine, but no spin-dryer; she relies on a mangle to extract surplus water. For many women readers, this story with its background of breast feeding, nappy washing and the struggle for identity when swamped in domesticity is a typical Margaret Drabble story and remains a favourite bringing out the acute Feminine Sensibility in her work.

In her next novel, *The Millstone* Drabble considers what it might be like to be a sexless virginal female. It is also a first person narration and is a story of Rosamund Staccy who gets a position in the university and is working on her Ph.D. thesis. She too dwells on the traditional, middle class, English morality and her life is largely defined and circumscribed by her present perception and values.

Rosamund stays at her parental flat with the parental atmosphere around her without their actual presence there. She dates with two men and each one thinks that she is sleeping with the other. In this way she avoids any close contact or sexual relationship with either of them. She is very much afraid of sex. She does not know the cause of this terror but blames her parents for installing this fear in her. However, in her first sexual encounter with George, who is a bisexual, she conceives. Her first, logical response to the discovery that she is pregnant is to have an abortion. But knowing more of books than of the world, she bungles her several attempts. It is here that the dilemma starts because her mother had brought her up as an equal and now that she was pregnant, she could not deny her femaleness and pretend that she was not a woman. In one of her outbursts she says:

> It would serve me right, I thought for having been born a woman in the first place. I couldn't pretend that I wasn't a woman, could I, however much I might try from day to day to avoid the issue? (*M.*, l6)

Rosamund directs her anger towards her parents because they had taught her to be aloof and remain withdrawn from everything because of fear of causing pain. This deeply affects the emotional responses of Rosamund because she is neither able to love nor hate spontaneously. Moreover, she is brought up with the typical middle-class notion of self-sacrifice so that when she finds out that Lydia her friend, with whom she is sharing her flat is writing a novel on her experience—at first, she is annoyed but is consoled by the fact that she is at the givers end and not a 'recipient.'

She continues throughout her pregnancy to find satisfaction in going on with her work. Her condition gives her an excuse to sever most of her social contacts and work more hours so that she thinks she may even finish the thesis before the baby is born. She sees no reason why her proposed career should be interrupted by having a baby. She says:

> I simply did not believe that the handicap of one small illegitimate baby would make a scrap of a difference to my career (*M.*, 94).

Apparently she is right because by the end of the novel, her thesis has been published, she has been offered a post at one of the most attractive new universities and she is embarked on a piece of work on Cowley and a chapter in a paperback survey of poetry. She is satisfied with herself. Nancy Hardin believes that all this goes to show that "Rosamund Staccy is basically a competent and self reliant young woman scholar."[3]

The *Times Literary Supplement* review of *The Millstone* began:

> The form of Margaret Drabble's cool and lucid novels is becoming familiar. She takes a clever, classy, arty but essentially self-contained modern girl and treats us to an exposition of her very reasoned and ordered inward musings....

This seems fairly clear and simple: Drabble woman is now a recognizable type with minor variations, the first person narrations inviting identifications with the author, who is known herself to be privileged and good looking and to share, to some extent, the problems of her narrators. The books all show humour, even wit but one does not know whether to take Sarah, Emma and Rosamund at their own valuations? Is the joke ever at their expense? Lucidity may be deceptive. Drabble makes her characters contradict themselves, even lie to themselves, whose voice is speaking, the characters, or the author's? The fascinated readers who identify with Drabble woman are comparing themselves, to some very odd fish.

The plot of the novel greatly changes with the birth of the baby. We find Rosamund insisting on her rights even if it involves screaming hysterically. For example, when her daughter is admitted in the hospital for a heart disorder and she is not allowed to see her. Rosamund feels the entire world collapsing round her. She feels restless, uneasy and is unable to sleep. In the end she can take it no more, so goes to the hospital and demands to see her baby even if it involves screaming hysterically. Formally she would not have behaved like this. As per her middle-class training she would have shown willingness to receive and take pains. But with the advent of the baby she learns or comes to see and appreciate the 'human lot' around her.

Even if Drabble shows this change in Rosamund, we find that she does not reach out to the people easily. She prefers to establish her own cozy world with Octavia. There is no room in this world for Octavia's father or for a husband because she wants to be free to bestow all her love on her daughter. Rosamund keeps aloof even from George and prefers not to tell him of his fatherhood. Its not that she does not wish to. In fact she longs in her heart to share this with George but controls herself because she is afraid of incurring a debt to him.

But, by coincidence as unlikely as the one which resulted in her pregnancy, she meets George in an all night drug-store. Actually she tries to avoid him but he comes to meet her and she invites him back for a drink and a look at her baby:

> 'You've got a baby, have you,' said George. 'I didn't even know you were married.' 'I'm not,' I said, and smiled, this time with true confidence; for here I was, safely back in my old role, the girl with alternating lovers, the girl with stray babies, the girl who does what she wants and does not suffer for it (*M.*, 136).

Here, we find Rosamund Staccy has achieved that desirable feminist synthesis Sarah Bennett aspired to. By remaining single she has established her independence, while through her motherhood she has affirmed both her flesh and her bonds with humanity. Nancy Hardin asserts:

> as a result of Rosamund's commitment to her pregnancy and subsequently to Octavia, she achieves a true synthesis both within herself and with the outside world.[4]

The Millstone marks a growth in Drabble's feminist consciousness because Rosamund successfully defines herself in relation to values other than the male superiority/female dependency ones of patriarchy.

While reading the novel, different opinions about Rosamund's behaviour are formed. Her complex relationship with her lover, her parents and her child, shows that she always maintained a distance and spoke only a part of the truth of what was going on in her mind. In an interview with Joanne V. Creighton, Margaret Drabble admits that she quite often does not have an analytical distance from her characters:

> I don't understand them. I wait and see what they do. I don't feel superior because I am sort of mystified; I present them with certain problems, which is the plot; the plot is the problem they are presented with, then they have to resolve it, and quite often I don't know whether I admit them or go along with them, or think they should have tried harder, I just don't know. As one does not know when a friend makes a decision; you don't know whether she should have left him or she should have had the baby; you don't know.[5]

Opinion varies from person to person. Rosamund though convincing and complying is judged differently by different viewers. However, her narration does create an impression on the readers but at the same time they lie open to multiple, divergent and inconclusive views.

In *The Waterfall,* the multiple, divergent and inconclusive interpretations reside in the narration itself which alternates between third and first-person points of view because the narrator, Jane Gray, cannot sustain the hypotheses she constructs without interrupting to lament the gaps. Jane criticizes her own story though it does not always satisfy the readers.

The Waterfall is a story of a love affair between Jane Gray and her cousin Lucy's husband named James. Jane is deserted by her husband, pregnant and about to deliver a child, she is living an empty life but suddenly her life takes a different turn after the arrival of a new baby and a lover.

Jane feels guilty about this affair because after all Lucy is her sister, so near in age and so alike physically and emotionally. In one of her narrations, Jane confesses that she always looked upto Lucy as an example because of the strong effect she had on her. She sees herself as being married because Lucy gets married and she sees herself as having children because Lucy has children. In all this she never for once thought about James because after all James was Lucy's husband. She denies this in her confession:

> It couldn't be possible that I wanted James because he was hers.... It wasn't so, it wasn't so (*W.*, 130).

The first person narration is self-justifying version of the 'real' and the 'true.' Jane is always afraid of rejection. She carries this feeling right from childhood to adulthood because of her mother's preference to her sister and rejection of herself. She marries Malcolm because he seems dependable and a safe man to go around with but one day this safe and dependable man bangs her head on the bedroom wall and deserts her. Actually, Jane strongly suspects Malcolm to be a homosexual but shuts and blames herself for the failure of the marriage. She confesses that she drove him out, by my bad housekeeping, by my staring at the wall, by my too evident frigidity (*W.*, 10).

And then her labour begins and she could hardly bring herself to summon the midwife, so reluctant was she to be seen. She delivers the child in a room made warm by electric heaters which the midwife had brought from the other rooms. Lying on her warm bed, Jane feels peaceful. Her cousin Lucy has come with her husband, James, to relieve the midwife and sit with Jane and her new daughter. After the first few days, Lucy returns to her house leaving James to spend the nights in the house with Jane.

Jane responds with passive enjoyment to his commands that she eat or drink or sleep. She takes his words as order and obeys them unprotestingly. And then when he tells her, he loves her:

> She flinched and sighed, alarmed and yet hopelessly moved by his willing blind suicidal dive into such deep waters; the

> waters closed over their heads, and they lay there, submerged, the cold dry land of non-loving abandoned (*W.*, 40).

Jane begins to live for his coming, submitting herself helplessly to the current of his passion for her and when the necessary six weeks after delivery are over, they make love. The previously frigid Jane is astonished that a desire so primitive could flow through her.

An abundant of birth imagery seems to surround the affair of James and Jane. In the first place, James is attracted to her largely because she has just had a baby. The fantasy that surrounds the novel is that Jane is the loving mother and the helpless infant. While reading about this fantasy the question that comes to the mind is that, what kind of mother Jane must be when she herself is playing the infant?

Jane's fantasy is romantic and is built upon fictional prototypes. A sleeping beauty's awakening by prince charming. The sleeping beauty lies all alone, exhausted by childbirth when she is found very beautiful by an attractive young man who is neither her husband nor the father of her child. He is an undemanding lover who waits patiently till she recovers from the childbirth and then he awakens her and a woman is born, not by his kiss but through sexual orgasm.

Jane fears that her life is imitating fiction and so she disdainfully proclaims that their affair is "some ridiculous imitation of a fictitious passion." She is confused by the fiction that is 'real' and the real that is 'unreal.' Thus, Drabble has shown that the relationship between fiction and reality is a problematic one.

The two voices in the novel are in the first person and third person. The third person is detached and tells the story only in a chronological order. It is a common technique used by the authors to convey a critical view of the characters, however, Drabble has used this technique in a slightly different way in the sense that whatever Jane narrates is in the first person and whatever she writes is in the third person so that Drabble is able to present alternately a selective account of the events in Jane's life.

The plot of *The Waterfall* recalls the plot of George Eliot's *The Mill on the Floss*. In both the novels, the heroine seems to undergo a moral and spiritual struggle. The characters of George Eliot created their own moral convictions and Margaret Drabble's characters seems to be doing the same. The ending, however, is different. Maggie never slept with her man and refrained from sexual indulgence but in the end had to die like so many heroines before her. But the heroine of Drabble boldly indulges in sex. Of course, the lovers do not marry and live happily ever after but they continue seeing each other accordingly. Drabble's heroines do not pay the price of death but they suffer either from thrombosis or neurosis and Jane might have died if she would not have stopped taking pills.

The water imagery used in the novel is symbolic of female sexuality. In *The Waterfall*, Jane Gray's first sexual orgasm is the 'Waterfall' in which she finds herself "down there at last in the water and not high up in my lonely place" (150) Jane drawn with James willingly in the sea of love. Jane finds love outside her marriage. Drabble interviewed by Olga Kenyon, talked of woman's writing as:

> Women have not thrown away the notion of the romantic novelist, who dealt with romance, the dark, stranger love.[6]

Out of traditional, even corny materials, Drabble weaves a richly symbolic narrative. On one level, Jane is a common place story of adultery. On another, it ponders creativity, femaleness, fertility and the nature of love. Drabble calls *The Waterfall* the most female of her books, and one can say the book which shows closely the Feminine Sensibility of Margaret Drabble.

The Third Person Narration

The four novels that have been discussed so far are written in first person narration. They are her early novels where the female protagonists face the crisis of modern life. They have been grouped together for convenience of study and to get a better view of her increasingly more sophisticated use of this narrative perspective.

The first novel written in third person narrative is *Jerusalem the Golden*, published in 1967. It was written before

The Waterfall. It seems different from her earlier novels, so far discussed, mainly because it is told in the third person. The narrator tells us the story of a good looking intelligent girl called Clara who cuts loose from her drab and repressive Northern background. Clara's search for life and survival takes her across a familiar British landscape, from Northern toughness and bareness to a more open but ambiguous world. Here we think it is a bit autobiographical because in her biography of Bennett, Drabble says she based the novel on her childhood memories of Sheffield: "I wrote the book from memory" (*A.B.*, 5). Like Drabble, the heroine of *Jerusalem the Golden* grows up in the barren territory of the industrial north of England. Her mother is both down and self-righteous or as Drabble has said of her own mother, depressed and depressing.[7] Nor surprisingly then, Clara views winning a scholarship to London University (as Drabble may have anticipated going to Cambridge) as her chance to escape to "some less obstinately alien world" (*J.G.*, 73). In her final year at the university, she finds that and more, "a truly terrestrial paradise where beautiful people in beautiful houses spoke of beautiful things" (*J.G.*, 37). She meets in short, the Denhams, a colourful and affectionate family, just the opposite of her own family.

In her interview with Drabble, Nancy Hardin observed:

> A significant characteristic of the young women in your novels is their inability to accept the values of their parents. Instead, they commit themselves to a search for 'chosen' or 'extended' families (friends, lovers or perhaps children) with whom they work through their identities and beliefs. Clara Mangham of *Jerusalem the Golden* comes to mind.[8]

Drabble's response is revealing:

> I have often wondered whether this problem is in particular to me in anyway, or whether it is a problem that afflicts almost all girls, and men too—that one has to escape from one's own family and find substitute families or substitute patterns of living. I don't know whether this might reveal my own family background. For many years my mother was very depressed. She's now not, thanks to, well quite

> frankly, thanks to drugs. So throughout my adolescence I was struggling with the fact that adult life seemed to be incredibly depressing...one had to find image of liveliness or colour or love that was different from what one had been brought upon. I don't know how I would have developed if I'd known my mother as she is now. She is so much more cheerful and active. I might have had a completely different view of needing to leave the family or having to find other mother figures...what one is looking for is just patterns of living in another people.[9]

Clara finds not only pattern of living in the Denhams' house but a lover too, in their married second son, Gabriel. Clara's mother has a house in a Northern suburb and Clara does not like the house at all because as she describes it, it does not have any warmth and openness, and the woman of the house, that is Clara's mother is a joyless person. No one ever visits their house and the cramped sitting room shows claustrophobic family and social life.

For Clara, normal family affection is as remote and unknown as the darker activities of humankind. Fifty years ago, British mothers were warned severely by experts of the dangers of 'spoiling' the children. Many mothers in those days, bent so far backwards as to be harsh. Mrs. Mangham tells the story of the Christmas stocking filled with ashes, as a lesson. This story is probably a folktale. Children had to be broken into a harsh world, taught that those who expected nothing would be disappointed. Mrs. Mangham tries to persuade her children that spending money is to be equated with 'vulgarity' and erects her own narrow prejudice into moral principles, with total lack of consistency or even rationality. She is a widespread British type undereducated, soured by disappointment, self-righteous, censorious, seeking cheap moral superiority in a bid for status. Mrs. Mangham is the kind of woman who turns down grammar school because uniforms have to be bought and Drabble has to wrench the plot slightly to permit this anti-intellectual woman who treats her daughter with venom and malice to let her go to Paris on a school trip. Mrs. Mangham grumbles about the expense but she takes a characteristic revenge on her daughter by making Clara wear a dowdy, cast-off party dress. The anguish of being forced to wear such a garment at the beautiful age of 16 is unimaginable. At every stage, Mrs. Mangham has derided and undermined her daughter. Instead of praising her good looks, she would only sneer and say, "Handsome is as handsome does."

Clara seems to be an unwanted child. She was named Clara, then an unfashionable name. She is christened out of a characteristic mixture of duty and malice. Clara's childhood is wretched. She has full of affection in her and nowhere to spend it. Even after getting to university she dreads the vacation because she has to return home to the trembling, silent, frustrated anxiety...endured throughout her childhood.

Clara is clever and intelligent. She decides to find a way for escape. She gets a scholarship and stays in London. Here she is regarded by others as smart and beautiful mainly because of her full breasts:

> She was naturally gratified by this change of front, and drew the appropriate moral...the possession of big breasts, like the possession of a tendency to acquire good examination result, implies power (*J.G.*, 46).

The possession of big breast enables Clara to have many boy friends and she cleverly chooses them as she wants to be acquainted with only those who have the ability to offer links and who are going to be useful to her. Here Drabble portrays the eager youthfulness of Clara for sophistication. The tremendous strain she undertakes to be the type of person she desires. Yet the world she seeks has an imaginative power set against hard realism:

> The world of the figurative was Clara's world of refuge. The literal world she inhabited was so plainly hostile that she seized with ardour upon any references made to any other being (*J.G.*, 32).

Clara is impressed by the hymn 'Jerusalem the Golden' because she pictures not a heavenly but a terrestrial paradise, where beautiful people in beautiful houses spoke of beautiful things.

At this point Clara happens to meet the Denhams who are exactly like the people of her dreams. She identifies with Clelia Denham who is beautiful, young, and her room is full of wonderful objects and reflects elegant living. In comparison Clara's room is bare and barren and she does not make any attempts to decorate it or possess it. It is like her mind totally empty and exactly the opposite of the Denhams. Gradually, Clelia becomes Clara's double and like Jane Gray of *The Waterfall* she sees herself in the identity of other woman.

Clelia's brother Gabriel is very much like her and the identity of Clara with Clelia leads her to sexually overtake the man. Clara sees no harm in this because he is so perfect in keeping with her golden fantasies. Gabriel's life is far from the heavenly fantasies of Clara. He has a wife and two children. His wife, Phillipia, is down with depression. His whole house and life is depressingly ramshackle and lacks the elegance of the house of his parents. But Clara prefers not to know all this and turns a blind eye and deaf ear to realities. She gets involved with Gabriel and, on their Paris visit, the reader is amazed to see Clara sleeping peacefully whereas Gabriel is worried about his wife, children and the servicing of his car. Of course, Clara is able to behave like this because she prefers to pretend not to know the harder facts.

In behaving like this, Clara is happy with life and pleased with herself. In doing so, she develops a rigidness and chooses a superficial world. Actually much of her energy is gone into escaping that which she did not know. This was a very inadequate way of looking at life. The novel remains open to varying judgements of Clara.

Throughout the novel we find that the narrator's attitude towards Clara is full of sympathy. Actually the story of Clara is that of a girl who longs for a world of larger imagination, more than real—the "terrestrial paradise" embodies in the title. So she leaves her mother's house. 'An oppressive mother' as many critics have described her because of her meanness and inability to love. However, ultimately we find that Clara ironically takes with her the very quality which she finds most disgusting in her mother—the inability to love:

> I am all nerve, I am hard, there is no love in me, I am too full of will to love... (*J.G.*, 165).

At such times along with the narrator, reader's sympathy too is evoked but one would have felt more sympathy for her if Clara would have been concerned more with her emotional barrenness rather than investing all her energy in the refusal of her past.

Margaret Drabble, in the author's comments very rightly points out:

> We are not free from our past, we are never free of the claims of others and we ought not wish to be.

Abandoning her mother to return to London, Clara gives up the possibility of true freedom, the ability to act creatively. Her declaration of independence, which concludes the novel, is an ironic revelation of how securely she is a prisoner of the fate she has created for herself:

> Her mother was dying but she herself would survive it, she would survive because she had willed herself to survive, because she did not have it in herself to die. Even the mercy and kindness of destiny she would survive, they would not get her that way, they would not get her at all (*J.G.*, 253).

The next novel of Margaret Drabble, *The Needle's Eye* (1972) deals with this very issue of the past. It has more characters and is dealt within a dense, moral, social and psychological context.

The novel surprised the readers because they thought it would be another novel about the situation of being a woman, but the first paragraph situates the reader in the consciousness of a man, Simon Camish, from whose point of view, most part of the novel is narrated. Talking to the reviewers, Margaret Drabble says:

> In *The Needle's Eye*, I've stepped rather nervously on to various floating icebergs, like writing at all about a man's job, which I have never dared to do before. And I had to work jolly hard to make sure that I got it plausible, let alone true and thats stepping out of one's limits.[10]

Perhaps that is why Drabble, prefaces the novel, to "all the lawyers who talked to me about this book."

The novel is built upon the reconnections and reflections of Simon and Rose who have each constructed a life set in opposition to their childhood worlds. Simon is a successful lawyer with a wealthy wife, a fashionable house and upper middle-class friends. He has cut himself off from his Northam working-class background. With Rose, it is the other way round. She has rejected first her wealth, then her parents and finally her husband Christopher to live with her children in a working-class district.

Simon has married Julie Philips. During his courtship, he thought he wanted to leave behind his mother's puritanical inhibitions by marrying a woman who represented to him: "Warmth, gaiety, vitality, family feeling, an easy affection; an easy enjoyment, all the things he had never hoped to have" (*N.E.*, 20).

But he is disappointed because Julie proves to be cold and superficial. Another major and more important turmoil in Simon's mind is the alienation he feels in the 'comfortable bourgeois texture' of the flat of his friends and also his own house. He constantly felt uneasy of the whole atmosphere and did not feel a sense of belonging towards the upper middle-class life in which he was supposed to be living happily with his family.

At times, he even felt strongly motivated to run to his mother where his true origin lay. He feels his whole life—the clothes he wore, the car he drove, the way he spoke, the house he lived in—was an act of misrepresentation. He feels that it is a corrupt way of living. He is full of self-contempt with a sense of being alienated from the upper middle-class.

He has grown up with a working-class background where the houses and rooms are small so that everything is cramped up. There is also a great deal of physical intimacy. When Simon grows up, he finds big spacious apartment as per the standards of his upper middle-class life but in this he feels the world of touch lost for ever and he feels "dry, dry as a bone."

Drabble portrays Simon as a man unable to reach out to the others, a man shockingly cut out from his children, who is finally resigned to passive endurance of the unsatisfactory life he has made for himself.

Valerie Myer feels that Simon is caught in a puritanical trap.[11] He wants to disinherit himself from his guilt and anxiety, especially as they take the form of social ambition. Yet he reveals in his perpetual rancour "an eternal human pattern of corruption":

> This is it, he would think to himself this I, doing what all men do, I am enacting those old and pre-ordained movements of the spirit, those ancient patterns of decay, I who had thought of myself different. I who had (surely) other intentions. Corrupt, humanly corrupt if not professionally so, and humanly embittered. And his spirit would struggle feebly within the net that held it, and he would imagine some pure evasion... (*N.E.*, 20).

There is it seems, no evasion for Simon. For him the past remains a net tenacious in its hold on him.

Rose has similarly strong associations to the past. As her name implies, she can experience to some degree a flowering, a rising, a transcendence of the present through a journey back to the past. Her middle name "Ventne" also points to the Christian symbolism latent in "Rose." As a young girl she felt herself to be Jesus Christ reincarnated (74) and as a young woman, she marries a man named Christopher, the 'Christ-bearer.'

Rose is harder to assess because she is seen through Simon's loving and sympathetic eyes. Like Simon, şhe is reacting against an unhappy childhood. This is mainly because her childhood nurse, Noreen, who is a religious fanatic has put into her head the evils of wealth. It is from Noreen that Rose learns to take literally the parable of the needle's eyes:

> about it being easier for camels to get through the needle's eyes than for rich people to get into kingdom of heaven (*N.E.*, 85).

Rose strongly believes what her nurse teaches her and so whatever she inherits, she gives it to build a school in an obscure African country, which ironically is burnt down a month later killing all the children.

In the beginning of *The Needle's Eye*, Rose and Simon meet at a dinner party and share their feelings of alienation from their homes, agreeing that it is sad but common to hate the place where one is born and does not wish to return. In the end, Rose decides to dissociate herself from the Bryanston estate in Norfolk which she tells Simon she hates even if she likes it too. She takes up a house in the lower middle-class section of London and feels hope for the future. Even though she felt uncertain at times she learnt to persevere etc.

Rose has built this "holy city brick by brick" and gets peace in it, but Christopher's calls disturb this mood and she thinks of Christopher's continuing hold on her as a punishment. At first, we see Christopher entirely through Rose's eyes as one who ill treats his wife. We cannot believe he married Rose for any other reason than her money. We hear about him only from Rose and like Simon, we naturally take her side. The plot becomes dramatic as Simon and Christopher begin to square off for a battle. When they meet at a party shortly after Easter weekend, Simon begins to see the bond that ties Christopher to Rose. Christopher is, in fact, Rose's spiritual counterpart, sharing her irrationality for more than which he has suspected all along, because to admit Christopher's sincerity is to believe that he did not marry for money and this in turn would force him to believe that Rose belongs to Christopher.

Suspense builds up and in a surprise move Christopher takes the children to Norfolk and Simon and Rose chase after him. After returning to her childhood home, Rose finds that she has suppressed her attachment to Christopher. She remembers a significant moment with him. On the last night she had slept with him in her parents house, when among the flowers in the garden she had felt transfixed by a silence and her blood had stopped flowing. Her discovery of sexuality with Christopher forged a bond with him. Therefore, she decides to remarry Christopher.

Many readers are surprised by this ending of *The Needle's Eye* but Drabble explains in The Author's Comments suggesting that Rose might have been mistaken in taking Christopher back and that they probably "would part again after another five years because she couldn't take it." But Drabble also asserts that the novel creates a logic demanding that Rose remarry Christopher.

In accepting Christopher, then, Rose is not affirming her most ordinary, functional self. She is simply substituting one of male authority figure for another. When Rose's spirit moves to accept Christopher, she imagines that "it might one day rise and reach and settle in the clearer air" (*N.E.*, 304). So Rose takes Christopher back to live with her but discovers to her dismay that "she had never made that leap into the clearer air."

Both Simon and Rose see her decision to take Christopher back as a denial of her self on behalf of "the others" (*N.E.*, 365) of Christopher and the children. But while this represents a religious victory to Simon, it is a religious defeat for Rose. She is waylaid on her journey to the boundary of patriarchal religion by a regressive detour to the centre of that primary patriarchal institution of marriage. Acting on response to Christopher's power, she denies not only her self interest but her self, her very nature.

Simon thinks that nature had made Rose "unremarkable, an ordinary person: fate had capriciously elected her to notoriety; and she had made the painful journey back to nature by herself, alone, guided by nothing but her own knowledge against the current" (*N.E.*, 299). Here, as so often, he is almost right. Her journey is back to nature, her own nature. But she doesn't make it all the way.

Simon always associates Rose with nature. "The images that gathered round her were emission, simple risings and gatherings from the soft, full lake of her nature" (*N.E.*, 175). So does Drabble, associating Rose with wild flowers, specifically with London Rocket, "a modest and unattractive little plant" that "grows on waste patches" in the big built cities that are man's 'improvement' on nature (*N.E.*, 218):

> 'I don't know what my images mean,' but I know they mean something fairly involved to me and I use them because I don't know what I mean in words.[12]

Perhaps because she doesn't quite know what she means to say about Rose, Drabble gives the task of explaining her to Simon, a man. *The Needle's Eye* might have been a very different novel had it been narrated from the point of view of Rose's friend, Emely, who recognised in Rose's collection of pressed wildflowers "her true history." Rose meets Emely when she goes away to school and even then the older girl intuitively understands when Rose tells her why she collects flowers:

> 'I did it for fun when I was six,' Rose confides, 'I was quite happy then I think. It got worse later.'
>
> 'Ah yes' said Emely, 'it does.... It gets worse and worse. You are quite right. You are the first person I've ever met who actually admitted it. But shall I tell your something? It doesn't go on getting worse for ever. There comes a point when it gets better and better. 'How do you know?' Rose challenges, and Emely answers, 'I know because I've made my mind up. I am not going to put up with it. You wait and see and you won't put up with it either' (*N.E.*, 222).

This is a woman's conversation in which much is said by being left unsaid. It is the life woman lives in patriarchal society, and as any woman knows, it gets worse and worse the older one grows. Emely mere radical than Rose, vows that she will not put up with it. And she hears she won't put up with it either. Collecting wild flowers, Rose is symbolically collecting and presenting herself from a patriarchal society which uproots all that is natural and replaces it with laws, institutions, cities and culture. At the end of the novel, Rose becomes, as Emely would see it, the final pressed flower in her collection.

Drabble's next novel, *The Realms of Gold* came out in 1975. In *The Needle's Eye* we find that the two protagonists of the novel Rose and Simon do not marry but in *The Realms of Gold* the central characters do marry and the end is happy. It is the story of Frances Wingate who has everything that one desires in life love, children and a professional career, but yet there are times when she is overcome by depression. Unlike her other earlier novels, this novel is full of characters. First, of course, is Frances Wingate, the heroine, then there is her cousin Janet Bud who is imprisoned with her small baby by her husband. Frances' nephew Stephen is not at all interested in life and so kills himself and his son. Then there is her great aunt Constance who has two illegitimate children but both the children die and also her adulterous lover and finally she also dies of starvation. There is cousin David Ollernshaw who lives a solitary and lonely life, which is a total contrast to Frances' gay and happy life. Then there is Frances' lover Karel Schmidt, his wife Joy; her mother; her father; her brother Hugh, his wife Natasha. All these characters act out and discuss an interplay of ideas. The main idea is the contradictory view between the modernist and the traditionalist—an essentially nineteenth century view of individual self-sufficiency and creativity versus a postmodern view of the overriding cultural, historical and social forces which shape the individuals. In this way, the novel functions as a dialogue between the traditional and the modern.

The first character, we meet, in *The Realms of Gold* is an octopus who lives in a square plastic box with holes for his arms. This mute creature speaks for the condition of all the principal characters of the novel. Frances Wingate, the central protagonist, loves the octopus she sees on her visit to marine research laboratory for its gray fleshy body, its lovely tinted iridescent gray muscles, its faint blushes and its grace. And she marvels that the octopus, an intelligent creature that it is, could survive in a plastic box.

As the novel opens, Frances Wingate, like the male octopus, is surviving rather nicely in a plastic box, which is how she thinks of her hotel room. But only temporarily. She never understands people who said that they felt submerged by hotel rooms, that they felt extinguished, annihilated, depersonalised, etc. She had occasionally felt the reverse—that herself, suddenly put down in transit, was so powerful that it might burst through the frail partition walls and send all the things swirling. Asserting herself, Frances—unlike Rose Vassiliou—makes it out of her plastic box all the way back to nature. And what she discovers there suggests that Drabble's vision in this novel is gynocentric.

The plot of *The Realms of Gold* has little to do with this vision. However, two observations can be made about the plot. First, at the beginning of the novel, all the principal characters are alone. Frances is divorced and her four children are rapidly growing to an age when they will no longer be dependent on her or living at home. She is estranged from her lover, Karel Schmidt, and her immediate family is hardly a close-knit one. When she is asked to fill in the column of next to kin on her travel and insurance form, she doesn't know whose name to put. Further, she thinks of Karel as the only man in Europe. The phrase is descriptive as well as complimentary, since Karel's family had perished in concentration camps. He alone of his generation had escaped. Frances' brother Hugh is isolated by alcohol. He drank at least half a bottle of scotch every night and if there was any thing to celebrate, he drank more.

Secondly, there are an amazing number of scientists in the novel. Frances is an archaeologist. Her father is a biologist, her mother a gynaecologist, her cousin a geologist. Her lover is an historian and a social scientist and Janet Bud's husband is a chemical engineer. These sciences and scientists can be categorised according to their attitudes towards life. Mark Bird, for example, is a futuristic technologist, who is attempting to improve on nature by inventing new kinds of indestructible matter. His idea of conservation is to agitate for the preservation of the town gravel pit as a children's playground. Lady Ollerenshaw is an ardent crusader for birth control and abortion law reform. She wanted more abortions, not less. Her husband, on the other hand, is a professor of zoology, a specialist on newts, which seem to Frances survivors from a world of pre-history, born before the Romans arrived.

The story is told by a narrator who is more of an observer because sometimes he is astonished by what is going on. For example, the narrator says that he had wanted David Ollerenshaw play a much larger role but state what the narrator also confesses of not being in control of the fate of the characters.

She admits, for example, as being torn between, "truth, likelihood and a natural benevolence." As the book expands, she is ready to admit that the fate of the characters is undecided.

By such confessions the narrator creates a rapport with the readers. The novel opens with Frances who like Clara Mangham in *Jerusalem the Golden* and Rose Vassiliou in *The Needle's Eye* has to return to her origin to discover who she is and find a way forward. This is an irony because Frances is an archaeologist whose profession is digging into the residue of other people and reconstructing their history from the evidence.

The archaeological learning in the novel is impressive. Frances has discovered a dead city called Tizouk. Here it is difficult to believe what Drabble writes because she says that Frances has discovered the city by fitting scraps of evidence and these scraps of evidence have come to her through intuition.... Now, when we are heading towards the 21st century and with tremendous scientific advancement it is difficult to believe that an entire city could be discovered through intuition. But, of course, one must not forget that this is a work of fiction. Ellen Cronan Rose is right when she says:

> I feel *The Needle's Eye* is essentially true and that *The Realms of Gold* is not only a work of fiction but fictitious.[13]

The story of two women run side by side, that of Frances and Janet. The main story is that of Frances. She is divorced and now is in love with Karel. But the problem is Karel is married and has children. However, unlike *The Needle's Eye* the end is a happy one as Frances's daughter Daisy marries Karel's son Bob and Karel's wife, Joy, turns into a lesbian and eventually decides to do a sensible thing and leave. Karel and Frances marry and are restored to happiness.

The story of Janet is sad one. She is a cousin of Frances on her father's side who lives an awful life on a housing estate with a mean and arrogant husband. Her only consolation is her baby. Desperately bored as a young mother and the wife of an insufferable husband, she is 'flattened out' by the landscape, so much so that at times she would admit to herself that she would have welcomed a volcano or an outbreak of war. Perhaps anything that could break the nothingness of her existence.

The novel foregrounds Frances, rich and famous while Janet Bud, miserable trapped housewife is relegated to the sidelines. At the end of the novel, Janet is bidding her time until something good happens to her, but it is hard to believe that anything will happen to Janet until it is too late. Janet's only hope is divorce and independence.

The novel is symbolic like *The Needle's Eye* but has a better plot and is written with more control. As Nora Foster Stovel says:

> Frances is free to choose gold or lead, survival or suicide, for both exist as surely as the pacific, but only a spirit as adventurous as Cortez can discover the golden realm.[14]

In a rich suggestive chapter, Susanna Roxman analyses the images of the novel—the landscape and vegetation which Frances and Karel observe from the car is 'half metallic and half dead'—and notes the integrated use of 'silver birches' in the passage. Ruminating on the theme of death, she observes that John probably drowned himself and that this sailor's end is a death by water. In her exploration of the earth, Frances the archaeologist, literally digs in the soil and eventually ends up digging her own garden; her grandparents had tilled the soil for a living. Roxman notes:

> there is earth as minerals, earth as mud or sand or soil, earth as vegetation, and earth as tilled land, giver of food. The earth is moreover a depository of riches, archaeological and geological.... We meet one earthquake inspector who claims to be in love with a seismologist. Finally earth is a place of burial...a metonymical symbol of death.[15]

Roxman points to the time aspect and kinship and reminds us that Drabble's vision of an ancient labour is compared to Wordsworth's Leech-gatherer and tells us that the fire symbolism in the novel is finely analysed. Roxman, observes that Janet Bud has characteristics traditionally ascribed to witches whereas Frances is linked to Queens.

The novel ends on a happy note. In an interview with Monica Mannheimer, Drabble admits:

> While Karel and Frances seem to have more freedom and spontaneity than Rose and Simon, these appearances of

> freedom and happiness can only be achieved by a lot of tricks in the novel.[16]

The tricks are that, there is no limit to the coincidences, which provide this novel's happy ending. Had it not been for the accident of a postal strike, Karel would have received Frances' summons to return to her rather in days than months. Since Karel had always promised that if asked, he would return. Of course, if there would have been no strike she would have been denied the opportunity of discovering her maternal roots.

The book sold very well in America. Drabble, the writer of feminine sensibility, has strongly brought out the character of Frances. In fact, it can be said that the character of Frances has been partly engineered to placate the feminist.

Drabble's next two novels *The Ice Age* (1977) and *The Middle Ground* (1980) deal with several features seen in *The Realms of Gold.* For example—the large cast of characters, the simultaneity of action and the omniscient narration. But at the same time it is different in the sense that the focus is not on anyone or anything in particular but has shifted to the general. *The Ice Age* deals with Britain, *The Middle Ground* with global problems.

Let us analyse *The Ice Age* very very briefly. Briefly because in this novel Drabble has focused her attention on a male character whereas all her other novels revolve round a woman as a central character.

As said above, *The Ice Age* deals with Britain—Britain suffering from an age of "ice." There is economic depression hanging over England combined with revolutionary terror. Margaret Drabble describes the state of the nation through the narrator:

> Those who had been complaining for last twenty years about the negligible rise in the cost of living did not, of course, have the grace to wish that they had saved their breath to cool their porridge, because once a complainer, always a complainer, so those who had complained most when there was nothing to complain about were having a really wonderful time now....

> There was, of course, a few perverse souls who enjoyed the prospect of a little austerity. They had been happiest during the war, and had returned to a life of cheese-rind-paring and carrot growing with alacrity....
>
> There were also the real poor, the old, the unemployed, the undesirable immigrants.... Let us not think of them. Their reward will be in heaven.
>
> Finally, there was the small communion of saints, who truly hoped that from this crisis would come a better sharing among the nations of the earth...they tried now to repress their horror and their satisfaction at the undefying spectacle of the death—threes of gred in their own so privileged nation (*I.A.*, 62-65).

The state of the nation is individualised in the fate of Anthony Keating, a property developer and son of the parsonage. Part one sets forth the depression troubling England in general and Anthony and his friends in particular. Part two defines a slow halting improvement in Anthony's physical and financial health. Part three presents Anthony as having found a faith in God. Part four asks why, if God is good, do evils exist. The fifth Part attempts to reconcile man's freewill and God's foreknowledge.

Thus, in short, we can say that *The Ice Age* is a struggle between God and man and ends with the search for God and the hope of spiritual renewal. The book ends with Anthony in prison where he plans to write a book about God. He watches the birds from his prison cell and thinks of them as the messengers of God.

Drabble has used the bird, both as a symbol of death and a human being. To quote Drabble in an interview given to Olga Kenyon on 25th January 1985:

> I knew half way through that I needed a bird at the end to resolve that particular shape. It begins with a pheasant, a large artificially-preserved bird, dying of a heart attack; this is a symbol of the death of the old culture. *The Ice Age* ends with a little rare bird that he sees while in prison in the Balkans. It symbolises the human spirit fluttering for ever in its rare and special way.[17]

The Middle Ground (1980) is radically different from *The Ice Age*. It is equally broadly focused upon a number of representative characters but once again Drabble's feelings about feminism are made a central focus in *The Middle Ground.* It is novel which combines an assessment of the condition of *middle age* with analysis of the social conditions of late seventies. In this book she makes feminism an explicit part of her subject matter and theme as a novelist.

Just as the phrase 'the ice age' triggers a cluster of related images for that novel, so also the title of this one imagistically focuses the work upon 'middle grounds'—some real, some figurative. It refers most obviously to the metaphorical 'middle ground' of life that is the mid life. The four central characters Kate, Evelyn, Hugo and Ted are all in middle age, successful in their profession and with grown up children. The figurative 'ground' upon which they had been standing seems to be a 'draughty open space' which is shifting and upsetting the old patterns. Meanwhile the actual 'ground' that is the environment in London is also going through a change. This change is shown through the main character Kate Armstrong.

Kate Armstrong is the heroine of *The Middle Ground* who is a journalist by profession, middle aged, divorced, an adoring mother, a successful newspaper writer on woman's issues. Through Kate's personal life, her social circle and her professional activities, Drabble produces a comprehensive survey of the contemporary circumstances of female existence in which sexual politics is prominent.

Kate writes about woman's issues and becomes very successful. We can say that she wrote them, at a time, just when "new wave woman's pieces" were in fashion. Just like Margaret Drabble's novels about woman came at the right time and became a hit. The negative side of Kate's situation is that as the subject of woman has become more and more fashionable, she has felt trapped and limited, and indeed bored by it. At the beginning of the narrative, Kate says to her friend Hugo Mainwaring that she is 'bloody sick of bloody woman' although she adds significantly that they won't go away just because she has got sick of them.

The topic of opportunities for women is pursued through Kate's activity in making a television film about the extent to which women's lives have been changed by the Sex Discrimination Act. What emerges is that for most of them, in a working-class area, nothing has changed, and furthermore that women are reluctant to say anything critical of men in front of a male producer and camera crew.

The television programme leads the interviewees into making fools of themselves, though—

> even if you had a female director, a female crew, a female television company with female managing directors and a female board, you'd still never get Denise Scooter to say a word in public against her husband, and not because she's frightened of him, but because she thinks it would be treachery. (And she would be right there also).
>
> Women's lives progress. What programme ought one to make, anyway? (*M.G.*, 80)

What indeed? The programme is called 'Woman at the Crossroads' but is referred to as "WC" by the men in control.

The novel ends unconclusively with Kate making preparations for a party which reminds us of Mrs. Dalloway's party. She explicitly imitates Mrs. Dolloway and sets off to buy flowers. In an interview with Cooper-Clark, Margaret Drabble says that this was a deliberate 'literary joke.' However, if we look further, we find that while Mrs. Dalloway finds her identity in her marital status, Kate is content to be single. While Mrs. Dalloway enjoys the uplifting texture of London life that is, the striking of Big Ben, the movement of the king through the city, the aeroplane overhead—Kate prefers to look down, "exploring her own weird shabby impossible sprawling unstylish noisy underground world" (*M.G.*, 185). Yet both Kate and Mrs. Dalloway are seen by close male friends, Hugo Mainwaring and Peter Walsh as vain and shallow but also beautiful and true.

A further comparison of Kate can be made to Virginia Woolf's Mrs. Ramsay in *To the Light House*. Like Mrs. Ramsay, Kate is connected intimately to the 'living house' that is the house in which she lives. Here, in a world of seeming disconnections, she generates a circle of connectedness and creating harmony. Like Mrs. Ramsay, Kate has brief moments of peace of seeing life steadily and seeing it whole:

> Looking around her family circle, feeling as she sat there a sense of immense calm, strength, centrality, as though she were indeed a centre of a circle, in the most old fashioned of ways, a moving circle—oh, there is no language left to describe such things, we have called it all so much in questions, but imagine a circle even so a circle and a moving sphere, for this is her house, and there she sits, she has everything and nothing, I give her everything and nothing (*M.G.*, 268).

The house in Drabble's work, as in Woolf's is an objectivisation of the self, an external expression of personality, and both writers are concerned with the relationship of this personal space to a larger and metaphysical connectedness. As in *To the Light House*, houses here are islands of the self in a seemingly hostile and indifferent world, one made all the more perplexing, jumbled and disorienting by the urban environment. Yet Evelyn and Kate observe that if one gets far enough above the cityscape, as from the scene from Evelyn's hospital room, the London scene seems not at all decaying and hopeless but varied, vital and self-renewing: reflective of a greater human connectedness:

> The old and the new side by side, overlapping jumbled, always decaying, yet always renewed; London, how could one· ever be tired of it? How could one stumble dully through its streets or waste time sitting in a leap staring at a wall? When there is a lay, its old intensity restored, shinning with invitation, all its shabby grime lost in perspective imperceptible from this dizzy height, its connections clear, its pathway revealed (*M.G.*, 238).

The novel undoubtedly has rich texture and metaphorical suggestions, one can conclude that *The Middle Ground* is a tribute to Woolf and the female experience and traditions that links them.

Drabble's next novel, *The Radiant Way* came out in 1987, almost seven years after *The Middle Ground.* During this time she was re-editing the Oxford Companion to English Literature. It is a novel, set at the beginning of the 1980's. The central focus is on three women in their mid forties. Liz is a psychiatrist, Alix is a part-time teacher of English at a prison and Esther is an art historian. All three of them are outsiders because Esther is Jewish, Liz is an outsider because her parents are Liberals.

Esther is in love with Clandio but all her efforts are in avoiding normal sexual intercourse. She believes that, "we are all very very sick" and talks obsessively about her potted palm, as if it were a pet. She may be doing this either to hide her emotions.

Alix marries young and has a son. She falls madly in love with the baby son so much so that she rejects her unsatisfactory husband. Fortunately, he gets drowned and Alix marries a socialist school teacher who has published a novel about working-class but failed to make progress.

The main character is Liz Headleand, the psychiatrist who has been divorced and in true Drabble fashion does not get an orgasm till she tries Charles her second husband. The novel opens with a new year's eve party in 1979 where both her husbands are present and Liz has the secret pleasure of knowing that two other men she has slept with are in the room.

Liz is a psychiatrist yet in real life, she cannot cope with her problems. She is distressed when her husband announces that he wants a divorce. They have been married for twenty years and have two daughters. At this point in mid-life, Liz wonders about her efficiency as a psychiatrist:

> I am as serviceable as ever. But how can I be, when I know that I do not understand my own problems, when I know that I do not know, when I have been obliged to admit that I do not stand on solid ground, when my own patterns are obscure to me? (*R.W.*, 80)

In this novel, we find one character viewing the other character and so along with our view we get the views of the characters themselves and come to know what they feel about a particular action or behaviour or a character. For example, Alix feels that Shirley exhibits "a habitual confidence." She admires Shirley's fashionable suit.

However, Shirley's sister Liz thinks just the opposite about the same suit and thinks Shirley looks ridiculous in it:

> Why was she wearing that department-store suit and that strange shirt with a watch-strap pattern and a big bow? It was hardly appropriate for an evening with old friends... (*R.W.*, 79).

The novel is not only about women's personal problems but it is also designed to survey British society going through a change. Drabble does this through a galaxy of characters several of whom are professionally in touch with social and political trends and have analytic skills.

While examining the British society of the 1980's Drabble produces pictures of times which Liz describes as 'mad' because of a polarization between the rich and the poor, closure of industries and withdrawal of educational provision. So though the novel is about women, it also concerns with problems that concern both men and women together. The novel ends with the three friends taking one of their habitual walks together in the country.

A Natural Curiosity (1989) is a sequence novel to *The Radiant Way*. The characters, of cources, are all the same but the three protagonists are separated. Liz remains in London, Esther has gone to live in Bologna. The main character in this novel is the third protagonist and the main plot concerns Alix's visit to Paul Whitmore who is a murderer and decapitator of women. The central mystry of the novel is that Paul, who lived in the same block of flats as Esther, is a mild mannered lonely vegetarian, perhaps because Paul's father is a butcher. Paul does not have a happy childhood. He has a twin sister who dies and Paul's mother abuses him for this and neglects him. However, Paul's father is a decent person and like the psychiatrist concludes that many children grow up fairly normal without any parental kindness or at least do not become murderers.

The three women represent three intellectual disciplines. Liz represents medical science and psychiatry, Alix English literature and Esther the art historian catalogues and interprets the iconography of a religion not her own. As said earlier Esther has gone to stay with Evelyn in Bologna but unfortunately she has to abandon Evelyn and return to Britain one does not know what to interpret. Is one to understand that she is renewed? Alix, the English teacher, starts wondering why she has spent so much of her adult life teaching in prisons and Liz gets into hot water by arguing on television that a pair of lovers, under 16, should not have been prosecuted, had they been left alone the boy would not have committed suicide. Then should one agree that sex between consenting underage school children is natural and healthy, as Liz argues on the television?

The novel ends with Brian finding inspiration to write another novel and the three friends go on a holiday to Italy. Jonathan Coe in the Guardian wrote:

> these novels are plunged into a flaccid half-way house between the realistic and the symbolic, fatally clouding any relationship which they might have enjoyed with the world upon which they are supposed to be passing comment.

One finds it reasonable enough to agree with Coe. After a brief survey of the major novels of Margaret Drabble, one finds that her works draw strength from literary context. It is also grounded in real experience, particularly women's experience and it is here that feminist perspectives are evident which strongly show Margaret Drabble to be a writer with acute feminine sensibility.

Drabble's early novels can be read as penetrating exposures of the female space. Elaine Showalter has called Virginia Woolf as the architect of female space, a space that is both sanctuary and prison. This can be seen in her *A Room of One's Own* where the women observe a violent masculine world. Woolf's vision of womanhood is very deadly. The ultimate room of one's own is the grave. Drabble's early novels are examples of such prototypically female spaces as well as struggles of women towards their own right. Her early characters are occupied with their appearance. Their houses are usually extensions of themselves, and protective retreats from external realities. These first person female protagonists are for the most part intelligent, educated and naturally fluent in the discourses of literature, psychology and contemporary culture. Yet their explanations of themselves are fragmentary and sometimes clearly inadequate.

Drabble's novels exemplify the tensions experienced by the contemporary women who are struggling to define themselves within a patriarchal frame of society. The strength of these characterisations, as has been seen, stems from her own unresolved questioning and her experiences of living in what she has termed the 'unchartered world' of modern female identity:

> We do not want to resemble the woman of the past, but where is our future? This is precisely the question that many novels written by women are trying to answer: some in comic terms, some in tragic, some in speculative. We live in an unchartered world, as far as manners and morals are concerned, we are having to make up our morality as we go. Our subject matters is enormous, there are whole new patterns to create.[18]

Drabble is a writer of feminine sensibility. She does not in her life or in her fiction advocate a feminist overthrow of the patriarchal order. Rather, she is a good-humoured realist, who mediates between 'male' and 'female' social, cultural and literary heritages producing a resonant fiction which is prototypically of her time, her place and her gender. She avoids being political and focuses on the inner sensibility of the twentieth century woman.

Drabble, perhaps more than any other contemporary British woman novelist, has the opportunity to produce a distinctly female work which surpasses gender limitations. She has said many times that she admires very much and strives to emulate George Eliot: for her range of subject matter, her social consciousness. Drabble mentions *Middle March* as a likely model for her next book, particularly its use of the omniscient narrator and the interconnected articulation of society—a kind of novel, Drabble has approached in her recent fiction. These broader, omnisciently narrated books of her later period—*The Realms of Gold, The Ice Age, The Middle Ground*—continue to be in many ways, double voiced, mediating, equivocal. Even when Drabble seems to be adopting traditional novelistic conventions, she is, in fact, adapting them, for she cannot reproduce the old sureties which often lay behind narrative conventions in the hands of eighteenth and nineteenth century writers. Drabble, in fact, knows this but uses it with playful and ironic detachment. Angus Wilson has perceptively said:

> She presses against the outer edges of the realistic mode with such respectful serious teasing...that the scruple or the hasty or the prejudiced...see only her competence, sincerity and readability and give only ordinary consideration to what we mistakenly class as ordinary work.[19]

There is a deeply personal honest and exploratory quality about Margaret Drabble's work. She confronts the unknown and acknowledges her limitations, so much so that at times one feels that she is muddling like her characters.

Drabble's fiction reflects the contemporary world in its complexities and uncertainties. Her early novels are a good deal more dense and more subtle than, at first, they appear. The surface lucidity of her novels and the technique of first person narration have led many readers to think that the persons of whom she is talking about are drawn from the author's personal life. This is an old problem with all the authors who write in the first person. However, this gives Margaret Drabble's work a hidden complexity distinguishing her from the other writers. From her very first novel, the depth and the subtlety of her first person characterisation grows, reaching its height in the portrait of Jane Gray of *The Waterfall. The Waterfall* is important because Jane Gray, the central female character, breaks out of the constricting bird cage of female identity shown in the first novel, *A Summer Bird Cage.* Her focus on the women's lives and her attempt to come to terms with women's changing role in modern society is serious, searching and important. Fundamentally liberal and humanistic, Margaret

Drabble is committed to the idea that novels should be alert common human experiences, as can be clearly seen in her writing.

Her earlier novels are in the first person narration and they all show her to be a traditionalist who does not want to experiment with the models of modernism and post-war experimentalism. As said in an interview, she prefers to remain at the end of a lying tradition. Her books are full of ordinary people and ordinary experience which directs her fiction towards realism. She engages with the reality of the character which makes her work deeply rooted in the line of British socio-moral fiction.

The study of Margaret Drabble's work is the study of the female voice. From her first novel, *A Summer Bird Cage*, depicting Sarah Bennett's indecisiveness about how to shape her life given the bird cage image of female identity she sees played out in the lives of women around her, to her latest novel, *The Middle Ground* portraying Kate Armstrong's paralyzing mid-life crisis in which no satisfactory pattern of how to live emerges, Drabble is seen exposing the social traditional avenues of middle-class female self-fulfilment, bringing out the feminine sensibility in her work. This reveals that Margaret Drabble indeed is a writer of feminine sensibility.

REFERENCES

1. Virginia K. Beards. "Margaret Drabble: Novels of a Cautious Feminist," *Critique*, 15, 1 (1973) 35-37.
2. Dee Pruessner. "Patterns in *The Garick Year,*" Schmidt ed. 117.
3. Nancy S. Hardin, "Drabble's *The Millstone*: A Fable of Our Times," *Critique*, 15, 1 (1973) 22-34.
4. *Ibid.*
5. Joanne V. Creighton. An Interview with Margaret Drabble in Doray Schmidt (ed.). Margaret Drabble's *The Golden Realms* (Edinburg, Texas: Pan American University Press, 1980) 29.
6. Olga Kenyon. Interview in *Woman Writers Talk* (Oxford: Lennard Publishing, 1989) 29.
7. Nancy S. Hardin. An Interview with Margaret Drabble. *Contemporary Literature*, 14, 3 (Summer 1973) 273-295.
8. *Ibid.*

9. *Ibid.*
10. John Clare. "Margaret Drabble's Everyday Hell," *Times*, 27th March 1972, London, 6.
11. Monica Lauritzen Mannheimer. The Search for Identity in Margaret Drabble's *The Needle's Eye, Dutch Quarterly Review* of Anglo American Lettes, Vol. 5, No. 1 (1975) 35-38.
12. Nancy S. Hardin. An Interview with Margaret Drabble. *Contemporary Literature*, 14, 3 (Summer 1973) 273-295.
13. Ellen Cronan Rose. *The Novels of Margaret Drabble* (London: Macmillan, 1989) 109.
14. Nora Foster Stovel. *Margaret Drabble: Symbolic Moralist* (Mercer Island: Starmont House, 1989) 130.
15. Susan Roxman, *Guilt and Glory*, 190.
16. Monica Mannheimer's "The Search for Identity in Margaret Drabble's *The Needle's Eye," Dutch Quarterly Review* of Anglo American Letters, 5, 1 (1976).
17. Olga Kenyon. *Women Novelists Today: A Survey of English Writing in the Seventies and Eighties* (Brignton: Harvester, 1988) 96.
18. Margaret Drabble. "A Woman Writer," *Books*, 11 (1973) 6.
19. Review of Arnold Bennett: "A Biography," *The Times* Literary Supplement, 12 July 1974, 737.

4

A War Within: Conflict in the Minds of the Woman Characters

As has been discussed earlier in this thesis the aims of feminist movements were initially economic in character. The early feminist demanded professions for unmarried women so that they could earn their own living. They also demanded the right to property for the married women. They backed up these demands by fighting for women's admission to universities in order to secure the qualifications necessary for their professional activities and to attain the level of education necessary to manage their own financial affairs. As their demands were conceded to and middle-class women began to move into professions, the feminist movement further demanded the right to vote.

In the course of time, women were given franchise but political equality did not ensure social equality, there was a note of disillusionment and betrayal that the free women were not free after all. They had profession and children but they were still bound to the husband, home and family triangle. There was a conflict between personal relationship and artistic integrity. Many young educated women had to fight with themselves in order to confirm their newly won liberation. Consequently, they had to experience a terrible war within. This war had claimed many precious lives. Women, in an attempt to assert their independent identity had to embrace death. Virginia Woolf and Sylvia Plath are two obvious examples.

Of all the contemporary English women novelists, Margaret Drabble has brought to the surface this conflict in the minds of educated women. She has a strong sense of obligation to female tradition. Her heroines provide a careful portrait of the contemporary woman with crisis and conflicts unknown to her predecessors. This is not to say that their personal conflicts are greater or any more frustrating, but they do reflect a much more complex engagement with the social and economic order.

In her first novel, *A Summer Bird Cage*, Drabble has shown the conflict of Sarah Bennett. She is the youngest of Drabble's heroines just graduated from Oxford with a first class honours degree in English. She is blessed with intelligence and good looks, but now after graduation she is caught in a conflict—marriage vs. career. She is exploring both the possibilities. None of the marriages she sees is encouraging. One is happy but dull, another exhilarating but self-destructive and a third, her sister Louise's, in which she had hoped to find a model of her own, ends in divorce.

Sarah is always caught in an inner conflict. She does not know what to do as a woman. The novel was published in 1963. At that time the educated or rather 'over educated' (because Sarah is an Oxford graduate) women lacked a sense of vocation. Sarah feels a classlessness and lack of commitment. Classlessness because she is not able to mix and belong to that class of women who are busy with their family. She finds a lot of difference between them and herself. She lacks commitment because she does not have a family of her own. She is unable to commit herself to marriage or career. Therefore, she takes a job with BBC and temporarily shares a flat with her college friend, Gill.

Sarah feels a pointlessness about her life because she has come to that stage where she has nothing to do. She feels her life is doomed because she is a woman. She is depressed over the shapelessness of women's lives and their vulnerabilities:

> I looked horrifyingly pregnable, somehow, at that moment: I looked at myself in fascination, thinking how unfair it was, to be born with so little a defence, like a soft snail without a shell. Men are all right, they are defined and enclosed, but we in order to live must be open and raw to all comers. What happens otherwise is worse than what

> happens normally, the embroidery and the childern and the sagging mind. I felt doomed to defeat. I felt all women were doomed (*S.B.C.*, 28-9).

As a young woman, Sarah has to decide whether she wants to be a grown up woman in a society that calls woman the second sex or remain aloof. She has ambivalent feelings about sex. So long as she can merely observe it, she finds it irresistibly desirable, but when she is invited to experience it she becomes frightened. For example, she thinks Lousie's lover is "stunning" but when at a party, he asks Sarah to dance with him she feels 'dazed,' 'squashed' and 'subdued.' She feels more comfortable with the man with whom she has come who kisses her arm intermittently and absent-mindedly.

There is a big conflict in Sarah's mind, she is attracted by sex and wants to experience it but, at the same time, she is scared. Since she finds it desirable, she has fantasies of exhibiting herself. She imagines her gown slipping off her bare shoulders, but then her bare body frightens her.

In Sarah Bennett, Drabble has dramatised the situation of the young girl, as de Beauvoir describes it in *The Second Sex*. She "wishes to be a child no longer, but she does not accept becoming an adult" because she enters adult life only in becoming a woman. The adolescent girl, she thinks:

> cannot become grown up without accepting her feminity; and she knows already that her sex condemns her to a mutilated and fixed existence.[1]

For Sarah, growing up means accepting her sexuality, yielding to biological imperatives, "the pulls of sex and blood." But as we have seen sex frightens Sarah. She does not want to be a sex doll but would like to be free to roam about in the world as Simone does, "through strange impermanent world where objects are invested with as much power as people, and places possibly with more" (*S.B.C.*, 75).

Sarah wants to be free to roam about in the world of the intellect and of art. This was the world in which she and Simone had lived during their days at Oxford. She wants herself and Simone to go on like that for ever. The conflict that Sarah faces is that she should either remain an irresponsible child as her days in Oxford or become a 'sexless' adult and although sex frightens Sarah, she is convinced that "the world of sensations is where I live" (75). Thus, Sarah is in the predicament de Beauvoir finds characteristic of the young girl. She does not accept the destiny assigned to her by nature and by society and yet she does not repudiate it completely. The conflict of Sarah reveals that she is a divided self.

In the next novel *The Garrick Year,* Drabble has shown Emma facing the same conflict. Emma is not able to resolve the conflict Sarah Bennett felt between her desire to become an adult woman and her wish to remain a child. Drabble reveals this by describing Emma's odd eating habits and her unusual attitudes towards food and eating.

While Sarah eats and drinks heartily, Emma only nibbles her food. Emma spends a great deal of time, when she is not dinning out, preparing and serving meals for others. She is shown breast-feeding her baby, cooking lamb stew for lunch and spaghetti for her husband's friends, cutting bread and butter for tea, frying innumerable pans of bacon and eggs, whipping eggs for mousse, etc. But we seldom see her eating, nor does she take pleasure in seeing others eat.

It is not that Emma is not interested in food. She is interested because at times she cooks a chocolate and even takes three helpings and enjoys over-eating. But this is very rare. Overall, there is a general disinterest in food and disgust with the act of eating. These are the symptoms of anorexia nervosa, which is an 'eating disorders' associated with a psychological problem, people misuse the eating function in their efforts to solve the problems of living which to them appear otherwise insoluble. Food lends itself readily to such usage because eating is always closely interlinked with interpersonal and emotional experience. Sarah's ambivalence about growing up, therefore, translates into a metaphor of eating, so also Emma Evans, who has an eating neurosis.

Mara Selvine Palazzoli, an Italian psychiatrist published a book in 1963, analyzing anorexia nervosa. Her findings corroborated in 1973 by Hilde Bruch who believed that many women who are slim, attractive and impress the general observer reveal under psychiatric exploration 'severe underlying psychopathology.'[2] These women, no matter how normal and even attractive they look, behave like anorexic, that is they suddenly and unaccountably stop eating. Emma Evans is such a woman.

The psychodynamic approach to anorexia nervosa sees the patients' attitudes towards food and eating as symbolic language. This is the language Emma speaks when she says she does not like steak. By rejecting the steak, Emma is symbolically and unconsciously rejecting sex.

Emma's conflict is the fear of sex or rather the fear of yielding to her own sexuality. She feels her body is getting away from her. It is no more under her control. It has become foreign to her. It has become a thing for others to see. On the street men follow her with their eyes and comment on her anatomy. When such a thing happens she feels frightened and would like to be invisible. It frightens her to be flesh and to show it to others. In short, she is afraid of sex.

Emma starts having a fantasy of sexless love. She dreams of Julian a young homosexual actor:

> I dreamed seemingly all night of Julian. It was an extraordinary dream, clearer than some of life itself. We were walking through Islington, Julian and I, and we were passionately in love. Islington itself was not the place I know it to be, but the place must once have been, with wide grass walks and fields and dandelions growing in the paving stones. It was as green as it now is stony, and I felt for Julian all that I had ever felt for anyone. I can remember it so distinctly, that image of breathless, exhausting, total admiring love. We had our arms round each other and I could even imagine in my dream what his thin girl's body would feel like to hold, so different from Wyndham's solid trunks or David's muscular torso; we were walking northwards from the Angel towards Islington Green and when we got there we sat down on one of the benches that bears the inscriptions 'persons not allowed to sleep on this seat,' and there we froze together in some immobile trance

> amongst the buttercups and the meadow sweet. It was like a scene out of a book, a passion out of a poem, it had all the pure intensity that never occurs in life, the dizzy undistractedness, with no rivers, no children (*G.Y.*, 202-3).

This sort of a dream would fulfil Sarah Bennett's wish to live on the emotional level rather than having actual pleasure of sex, yet Emma dreams this because Julian is a homosexual and so they can have sexless love. One question that comes to the mind, here, is that if this is the conflict of Emma—then why does she marry David and have two children by him?

Emma was attracted to David not because of his personal attributes. In fact she disliked them. She marries him because as she puts it in her own words:

> With him, I felt that I was on the verge of some unknown and frightful land, black desert, white sand, huge rocky landscapes, great jungles of ferns (*G.Y.*, 112).

This landscape has nothing to do with the plot of the novel. It is psychic. What Emma feels is her own sexual urge and her body responding to it. So she marries David and has children. But Emma develops a conflict and fear of responding to her own sexuality because she feels the same about Wyndham, so she finds it convenient to dream about Julian where sex would not be involved at all.

But one day Julian drowns himself in the river Avon. On the symbolic level, to drown means to yield. The drowning of Julian represents his acceptance of his homosexuality. But Emma will not accept her strong desire for sex she says:

> You will not find me at the bottom of any river. I have grown into the earth. I am terrestrial (*G.Y.*, 219).

Like Sarah Bennett, Emma wants adulthood on her own terms. She wants marriage but does not want to fulfil her conjugal obligations. She wants motherhood, but she does not want to breast-feed. And she wants sex, but only from the waist up:

> Kissing I did not mind: in fact, I soon discovered that anything above the waist, so to speak, I did not mind, but anything below was out of the question (*G.Y.*, 164).

The conflict of Emma is the same as that of Sarah. She wants to both, grow up and remain small. How can this be possible? Another conflict she faces is that she has a strong desire for sex but she does not like the 'mess of the union.' She wants motherhood and marriage but is "appalled by the filthy mess of pregnancy and birth." She is impatient to wean her baby because she says, "my breasts are too big." She habitually sees herself to be self-divided. She has given up the chance of a career as a television news reader and so many other things for the sake of marriage, she muses:

> I could hardly believe that marriage was going to deprive me of this too. It had already deprived me of so many things which I had childishly overvalued: My independence, my income, my twenty two inch waist, my sleep, most of my friends, who had deserted me on account of David's insults, a whole string of finite things, and many more indefinite attributes like hope and expectations (*G.Y.*, 10).

Thus, one can see that as with Sarah, there are disturbing anomalies in Emma's view of herself. Rosamund Staccy, the central woman character of Drabble's next novel faces the same conflict. She wants love without sex. In her college days she has a boy friend named Hamish. With him it looks as if she is having an affair while actually she is abstaining from sex. Although she and Hamish spend nights together, in hotel rooms, they do not make love. But after Hamish leaves, she cannot find a lover fulfilling her orthodox need so she devices a strategy. She dates two men at a time making them each think she is sleeping with the other. In making this arrangement, Rosamund gets what she wants. She gets the masculine company which she enjoys but at the same time she can avoid sleeping with them.

The conflict with Rosamund is that, she wants love, she wants touch but she does not want contact. How can this be possible? However, she dates and makes friends with George Mathews, whom she thinks is a homosexual. She spends a night with him and allows him to make love thinking him to be homosexual but gradually she is so much overcome with sexual desire that she cannot avoid the final touch and thus conceives.

Rosamund's unique sexual encounter is an accident and this leads to further conflicts in her life. Rosamund had always been a very independent person but now she feels her independence threatened:

> I saw that from now on I...was going to have to ask for help, and from strangers too: I who could not even ask for love or friendship.... I could feel my own personal morality threatened: I was going to have to do things that I couldn't do. Not things that were wrong, nothing as dramatic as that, but things that were against the grain of my nature (*M.*, 72).

> Rosamund has an easy childbirth and compromises her independence only to the extent of accepting free help from Lydia and paid help two days a week from an amiable lady while she goes to the library to work.

Rosamund's independent nature and her unwillingness to accept help from others is the result of her upbringing. She has been taught such facts, such withdrawal, such fear of causing pain, such willingness to receive and take pains that she cannot reach out openly to other people. She fears that nobody would want her or that she would be tedious. Her conflict is:

> In case I am not wanted. In case I am tedious....

Her parents' characteristic self-denial and self-sacrifice has been picked up by Rosamund. But this has caused a great conflict and suffering in her life because she is unable to accept love. There is a fear in her of incurring a debt to others or of being unfair. Part of her attitude also stems from her mother's valuing of female independence so that Rosamund, in trying to be equal, tries to deny the womanliness in herself she tells us:

> My mother, you know, was a great feminist. She brought me up to be equal. She made there be no question, no difference. I was equal. I am equal (*M.*, 28-9).

She is shocked to realise that she is pregnant because she had denied femaleness to herself. This creates the essential conflict which leads her to believe that she is a woman as it is useless to pretend otherwise:

> It would serve me, right, I thought, for having been born a woman in the first place. I couldn't pretend that I wasn't a woman, could I however much I might try from day to day to avoid the issue? (*M.*, 16).

During her pregnancy Joe wants to help Rosamund. He is not interested in who the father is but since he likes Rosamund, he wants to help her but Rosamund is unable to accept his love. On the other hand, she wants to get rid of him as she is too proud and does not want pity or kindness from him.

Rosamund suffers from spiritual poverty as she is not able to accept love even if she wants to. She prefers a life of isolation. However, she realises that she will necessarily have to involve herself with other human beings. So far she had successfully avoided any bond that linked her deeply with any other human being. She had successfully avoided George but now she could not avoid her own child. It was going to be her own flesh and blood. A strong bond was going to tie her up with the child. As it will be seen later, Rosamund spends many a sleepless nights and many moments of anguish, which link her so closely with the child.

Rosamund has finally realised the limitations of her life and she learns to live within these limitations. Like Emma, she prides herself on her ability to place mind over matter but now for the first time she has no control over her body, like an anorexic, she wants to turn her back on what is imposed on her. Mara Selvini Palazzoli, an Italian psychiatrist explains that a girl suffers from anorexia when her body undergoes a change during puberty. This frightens her for two reasons. First, they remind her that she is biologically doomed to play a passive receptive role. And second, there seems to be nothing she can do about it. It is this fear that makes Rosamund remark that it serves her right for having been born a woman. Here Drabble brings out the helplessness of a woman who finds herself alone in the world that surrounds her. Situations like these make Drabble a staunch feminist who concerns herself with the feminine experience and feminine sensibility.

Once the baby is born, a part of the conflict in Rosamund's life ends and a new one begins. For the first time in her life, she is introduced to love, the love she feels for the baby, and the miraculous and uncritical devotion that Octavia gives in return. In many ways she desires to establish with Octavia a cozy little world of the two because Octavia's love was uncritical and she could freely bestow her own love upon her.

Susan Spitzer in her article, "Fantasy and Femaleness in Margaret Drabble's—*The Millstone*" says that Rosamund's baby can be viewed as a fantasized replay of the loved and loving parents child union of which she is deprived.[3] She is right when she says this because Rosamund has a very unhappy childhood and has an anger towards her morally scrupulous parents who have always taught her self-denial and self-sacrifice and not true love and spontaneous friendship.

Although Rosamund has an easy childbirth, it is found that Octavia has a fatal heart defect demanding immediate and extremely risky operation. The night before the baby is admitted to the hospital Rosamund experiences a conflict within herself. She lies in an agony of anxiety and emotion, Margaret Drabble is able to combine the two sides of her nature, the academic and the maternal. Rosamund is doing Ph.D. on Elizabethan poetry. Suddenly, her Elizabethan poetic imagery shifts from the library to the heart revealing her conflict:

> Towards morning, I began to think that my sin lay in my love for her...Ben Jonson said of his dead child, my sin was too much hope of thee, loved boy. We too easily take what the poets write as figures of speech, as pretty images, as strings of bons mots. Sometimes perhaps they speak the truth (*M.*, 127).

But the final crisis comes after the operation. Conflict between love and self-denial begins. Rosamund has been taught self-denial and self-sacrifice. She was always at the givers end. But now these philosophies of life had to be thrown aside because it was too strong a force for Rosamund to deny it. For two weeks she was not allowed to see the baby in the hospital.

This made her impatient. She must see Octavia. All her dislike for fuss and dread of inconveniencing others disappeared:

> This time I felt that I would not be the only one to lose; somewhere Octavia was lying around waiting for me. It was no longer a question of what I wanted: this time there was someone else involved. Life would never be a simple question of self-denial again (*M.*, 6).

Here, during this suffering and conflict we find that the doctrine of self-denial which was imposed on Rosamund by her parents is put aside by the demands of love for the child. Rosamund realises that this is the moment of psychological resolve, as intellectual understanding and deep honest feelings fuse into a whole. The experience is worth quoting:

> Inside my head it was red and black and very hot, I remember, and I remember also the clearness of my consciousness and the ferocity of my emotion, and myself enduring them, myself neither one nor the other, but eduring them and not breaking in two (*M.*, 134).

This is not the end of the novel but it is a climax. Drabble has convincingly brought out Rosamund's sense of independence, competence and self-reliance and her attempts to avoid her existential vulnerabilities as well as her need for other people.

So far it has been noticed that Sarah, Emma and Rosamund, Drabble's heroines of her first three novels, have conflict regarding sex-experience because they believe that yielding to its 'important pulls' will condemn them. They also sense that their identity as women is profoundly connected with their sexuality. However, Jane, the heroine of *The Waterfall* is entangled in a different conflict. She does not deny her female identity. On the other hand, she enjoys the warm dampness of the room in which she gives birth to her second child. She lets her sweat and her blood flow without embarrassment or distaste and likes the thin warm wetness of the tea offered to her by the midwife. Jame compares the tea with weeping because both are warm—the tea and the tears. Jane has given a birth to a child. The delivery is over but in the process she is herself 'Delivered.'

Delivered, here does not mean the usual word, that is giving birth. But it means setting free from rescue or release. Here, in this case, James makes love to Jane and releases her sexual, womanly self.

Jane is that Drabble woman who is struggling to find a new morality. The novel *The Waterfall* centres on the love affair between Jane Gray and her cousin Lucy's husband James, and Jane's ambivalent and conflict-ridden views of the affair.

The conflict with Jane is that she is divided between the 'two selves' within her—that is Jane Gray the woman and Jane Gray the artist, for Jane Gray is a writer who writes and publishes poems. As a woman she is experiencing sex, fulfilment, femininity and as an artist she tries to give form, order and shapeliness to that experience.

Jane Gray, thus, plays two roles: woman and the woman artist. As a woman she acknowledges the existence within herself. She does this by discovering with James her essentially passive sexuality. But she does not remain in sexual bondage to James. Towards the end of the novel she reasserts the artist in herself, has written a very good sequence of verse and has published it. Initially there is a clear division between the 'I' who meditates the art of writing and the 'she' who has a love affair with James at Oxford. But towards the end of the novel these distinctions blow. Finally the 'I' and 'she' come together. That is the third person narrations ends and switches to the first.

This signals the unification of Jane Gray who was early a divided self.

Although the woman and the artist in Jane unite, yet the conflicting views of Jane about her affair with James remains. Although she is sexually liberated, she finds the affair to be immoral, trivial fantasy with disturbing and largely unexamined psychological implications. Fantasy because the entire love affair starts in the manner of a fairy tale with Jane as the Sleeping Beauty lying all alone in a bloody childbirth when suddenly into her life comes a gentleman who is very attractive. The man is neither her husband nor the father of the baby. He becomes her lover and he waits patiently till she recovers from her childbirth and then they make love. The entire story reads like fantasy.

It is during this love-making that Jane is reborn and a woman is delivered because for the first time she is 'awakened' through sexual orgasm. Although this is a unique experience for Jane setting her free from her sex starvation yet this experience is accompanied by doubts and fear. Since the entire experience is like a fantasy tale Jane fears that their affair is some ridiculous imitation of a fictitious passion. Jane is perplexed by fictions and fantasies that are 'real' and by reality that is 'unreal.' Her love affair has given her James but she is unable to describe it to him. What can she call such a possession who is someone else's husband?

> Which was Charlotte Bronte's man, the one she cared and wept for and longed for, or the poor curate that had her and killed her, her sexual measure, her sexual match? I had James, Oh God, I had him, but I can't describe the condition of that possession: world that I lived in with him —the dusty Victorian house, the fast car, the race tracks, the garages, the wide bed—it was a foreign country to me, some Brussels of the mind (*W.*, 84).

Jane struggles in her relationship with James. She enjoys every minute with him but morally she is upset. But she also feels her affair is a preordained 'miracle' and 'amazing fate' which saves her. Saves her because, after her husband Malcolm leaves her in the seventh month of her second pregnancy, Jane retreats into total isolation. As her first child is staying with its grandparents, she has no reason to leave her house and doesn't.

At this time, when Jane is in total isolation and in tremendous need of love and humanity, James comes into her life like 'prince charming' from a fairy tale. In this relationship Jane was hoping as she says, "to find some kind of unity" but things are destined quite differently and they meet with a serious car accident. According to the rules of fiction, Jane should have died because all true fictional lovers die. But she doesn't. Jane feels the accident is a punishment for her immoral behaviour.

Jane wishes that both of them should have died in the accident but now that they are alive their lives will be lingering bringing frustration. If they would have died, all the bitterness and conflict would have been wiped away. Whatever the consequences Jane Gray is a very lucky woman because she is able to fulfil a number of roles particularly assigned to woman: she is wife, mother, mistress and housewife and also an artist. Drabble in an interview with Nancy Hardin calls *The Waterfall* 'a wicked book' because it describes an experience "that is not universal but the experience of sublime romantic passion."[4] She has also called *The Waterfall* "the most female of all my books."

At the end of the novel Jane's conflict remains—she remains torn between her tragic love and her morality. It is a character struggle. A struggle over the passion and efforts at self-consciousness. Yet, in the end, she is able to carry on contentedly with life as she could not before: cleaning her house, nurturing her children, visiting her in-laws, writing and publishing poetry, talking with her literary friends, seeing James occasionally and expecting to see Malcolm sometime. The ferocity of the conflict perhaps decreases, is all that can be said.

From Jane Gray we now move to the conflict of Rose Vassiliou who calls herself "an ordinary person." Rose has been struggling through legal nightmares all her life. When she was twenty, her parents made her a ward of court to prevent her from marrying a Greek from Camden Town, whose parents ran a travel agency and smuggled Greeks out of Cyprus. The day after her twenty first birthday, she married him and was promptly disinherited. Eleven years later, she divorced him for cruelty and as the novel opens, she is again involved in legal battles as her divorced husband, Christopher, wants the custody of their three children. Actually, Rose is tremendously scared of lawyers. She comments to Simone, her friend, "I am terrified of lawyers" and Simone understands this because he remembers how her face had 'flickered and flinched' when she found out that he was a barrister.

The conflict of Rose with Christopher reaches the halls of court and because of Christopher's actions, Rose needs a lawyer and she turns to Simone for help. Simone comforts her by saying that the court will consider whether Christopher has adequate accommodation for the children because according to him the law took serious view of things like accommodation.

Rose suffers because of Christopher's attitude. His case rests on the contention that Rose, who lives in a decaying house in a working-class neighbourhood is depriving his children of material benefits. She reflects on the spiritual benefits in living as she does. But the conflict in her mind is, "what sort of defence would this make in a court of law?"

Rose is so fed-up and tired by the rules and regulations of law that she decides to give up the custody case. In taking this decision there is also a moral conflict within her and is convinced that Christopher is right. She feels she is being very selfish in not allowing the children their father. The moral conflict is worth quoting:

> I am a hopeless mother, I know I am, I'm mean and mad and selfish, he's right about me, how can I defend myself when he is right (*N.E.*, 255).

While this conflict is going on in the mind of Rose she receives a telegram from Christopher saying that he was abducting the children out of the country. By this time the judgement of the court has also arrived and she has won the case. But she is not able to celebrate the victory. It was a fight in which there was no winning. Christopher had taken away the children and she was worried.

Rose does not accept victory nor does she accept the verdict of the judges. She solves the matter by her own moral standards. She decides to remarry and live with Christopher so that they both could have the children.

Like Rosamund, Rose also believes in the doctrine of 'self-denial' and to go with it was her conflict of religion. Rose seems to be attempting to create on the boundary of Christianity a non-hypostatic religion, in which religious experience is not a relationship between herself and a personification of transcendent otherness, but a realization of the creative potential for being within herself.[5] This conflict has been put in her by her governess, Noreen, who is a religious fanatic who puts into Rose's head the evils of wealth. From Noreen, Rose learns to take literally the parable of the needle's eyes, "about it being easier for camel to get through the needle's eyes than for rich people to get into the kingdom of heaven"—of belief that leads her to give away her inherited wealth to build a school for the African children. Her religiosity is mixed with inescapable conflicts and so in her marriage to Christopher. When she gives away her wealth she enjoys the sense of moral purpose it gave her but at the same time she admits the fully to which it led.

Rose marries Christopher for two reasons: first, to escape the conflict of Noreen's religiosity and secondly, to escape the conflict of her parents' materialism. But unfortunately her marriage to Christopher itself becomes an additional conflict because she soon finds out that Christopher was no different from her father who uses somewhat shady practices to rise from rags to richness in his business. To escape these family conflicts she takes up a house on Middle Road based on her religious values of simplicity where she finds peace and an escape from her marriage and parents' materialism. She calls this small house her 'holy city' where she dreams of a vision of renewal:

> a hope for the future: she shivered, she trembled, she flinched, but she preserved, she had faith she built up brick by brick the holy city of her childhood, the holy, the holy city in the shape of that patched subsiding house (*N.E.*, 53).

In her new house she achieves happiness in her isolated moments and through careful work and great patience achieves reality and a 'visionary peace.' But Christopher calls and disrupts the mood of peace Rose has found. The conflict once again begins. She thinks of Christopher's arrival as a punishment for having thought that she could be happy. And now she no longer was. She thinks often of Christopher's continuing hold on her and on the children as 'a penalty.' Noreen disturbed her peace as a girl and Christopher disturbs her peace as a woman. Because of these two people a conflicting battle starts in her mind and she starts feeling guilty and undeserving and thinks of her happiness as a crime. Although they are divorced, she is not able to get rid of her sense of guilt:

> That dim surging and conflict within her when she thought of him and what they had been through together could not be parcelled out or judged or ended by any means but its own. In its own place it must be decided (*N.E.*, 181).

Women are more religious minded and moral conscious than men. It is exactly so with Rosamund which makes her a character of Feminine Sensibility. Rose feels her conflict cannot end in any way so she decides to withdraw from the field of conflict, in this way she will also silence the voices of her religious battle. She decides to take Christopher as "regressive capitulation to the 'patriarchal institution' of marriage, a female denial of self in response to his male power." She is right when she says this. After all, she is a strong feminist. But, self-denial is one of the attributes of feminine sensibility, very typical like Rosamund, the heroine of *The Millstone.* Both the woman characters of Drabble not only show the same characteristic of self-denial but the author has also used a great and very close similarity in their names also. Both of them face moral conflicts and both their names are closely linked to religion showing and bringing forth various meanings. According to J.C. Cooper's An Illustrated Encyclopaedia of Traditional Symbols, the rose is:

> ...a highly complex symbol...ambivalent as both heavenly perfection and earthly passion...time and eternity, life and death, fertility and virginity...perfection...completion; the mystery of life; the heart centre of life...beauty, grace; happiness, but also voluptuousness...wine, sensuality and seduction.
>
> In the symbolism of the heart, the rose occupies the central point of the cross, the point of unity. As the flower of the feminine deities it is love, life, creation, fertility, beauty...death, morality and sorrow; its thorns signify pain, blood and martrydom...it portrays eternal life, eternal spring, resurrection...it is the flower of venus and the blood of...Christ...the Rose Garden is a paradise symbol... Alchemic: the rose is wisdom...there birth of the spiritual

> after the death of the temporal...the flower of paradise... from the drop of Christ's blood on cavalry...the centre of the rose is the sun and petals the infinite, but harmonious, diversities of Nature. The Rose emanates from the tree of life, which implies regeneration and resurrection.[6]

All these meanings are applicable to the character of Rose within the novel. Her first appearance associates her with ancient religious verities:

> She looked, because of age and softness authentic, as ancient frescoes look in churches, frescoes which in their very dimness offer a promise of truth that a more brilliant (however beautiful) restoration denies (*M.P.*, 27).

Thus Rose's name is full of symbolic meanings and Drabble attributed most of those qualities to her characters that go with the meaning. However, when she decides to take Christopher back Marion Vlastog Libby concludes, "A female trapped once again with a hostile man."[7] Rose does not take Christopher back for her own happiness but for the good of whole family. There are every chances that she may again divorce him, but by then the children would have grown up and perhaps they would be able to fully understand her. The author herself comments, "they probably would part after another five years because she couldn't take it." Till then Rose's conflict and suffering in marriage continues. But Frances, the leading character of *The Realms of Gold* is assertive and different from Rose Vassiliou. She frees herself from the family tangle and conflict and turns all the way back to nature and what she discovers there suggests that Drabble's vision in this novel is gynocentric.

The problem and conflict of Frances is her depression and loneliness. Lying alone in a posh hotel room where she is the star-speaker of a conference she thinks and contemplates and compares herself with an Octopus which she has seen in a marine research laboratory. Frances is aware that female Octopods dies after giving birth. She herself has given birth four times and now wonders what else she is for. Taught to look on her miseries as cyclic, Frances, like Jane expects revelation. Tranquillizers have had no effect. This is because she is not good at following instruction on bottles, or waiting for cumulative effects.

The conflict in France's mind is intense because she is haunted by the memories of the past. Presently she is in the city in which she had stayed with Karel her lover and had finally parted from him. She somehow finds herself responsible for her fate:

> ...something of a salvationist, he had wished to save her, with evangelical passion and she was afraid of disappointing him...so she had told him firmly that she was mad and beyond redemption....
>
> While not quite able to accept the theory of penis envy, she was more and more convinced that what every woman wanted was a man, and that what every man wanted was a woman, or that if they didn't want that they ought to, and that the only possibility of happiness and harmlessness on earth was to be found where Freud would have us find them (*R.G.*, 29).

These things come to the mind of Frances one by one. The real problem is that Karel, France's lover is married. France's own marriage has been grim and violent; it has hardened her, as isolation hardened Rose.

The conflict in Frances deepens after bidding adieu to Karel. Her heart becomes very heavy. She tells her brother that she feels as though she has got a terrible stone in her chest. This is all because of the loneliness; she misses Karel desperately. Her grief increases day by day and she feels her heart so heavy, as though she had swallowed a stone. She turns weekly to her family because she has no real friends, only colleagues and acquaintances.

Frances comes out of her isolation. Her first step is to visit her parents and brother. She decides to find out about her ancestors. As she investigates, she finds that Ollerenshaw's family history is far from cheerful. She finds out that there is a hereditary disease in the family—the disease of depression. And until the action of the novel begins, Frances has been fairly successful at warding it off:

> She has learned to deal with it, by denying its significance: she had refused to take it too seriously, but had it sweat itself out like a dose of malaria. She had clung to activity and movement as an escape, and on the whole her remedy had worked: she had been able to evade the effects of the sickness if not the sickness itself (*R.G.*, 97).

The novel opens with Frances suffering from an attack of depression. She endures the symptoms of nervous breakdown. Like Clara Mangham in *Jerusalem the Golden* and Rose Vassiliou of *The Needle's Eye*. She has to return to her origins to discover who she is and find a way forward. This is an irony because Frances' profession is digging into the residues of other people and reconstructing their history from the evidence: bones, teeth, artefacts.

Frances works hard to ward off misery, which as she says leads her relatives to suicide, drugs, drinks and madhouse. Her head feels like 'askuel.' She thinks of herself as "in the middle of nowhere, high up a solitary lunatic, in her dry creater." Her cure for pain is to repeat to herself poems of Milton and Wordsworth, which she has used to help her comply her husband's desire for sexual intercourse and which she had shouted aloud in childbirth so she recites poems of Wordsworth and Milton. It is clear that her pain is not merely physical.

Frances also conflicts with Matrophobia that is the fear not of one's mother or motherhood but of becoming one's mother. Frances does not want to become like her mother because she considers her very unmotherly and feels herself very much unmothered and a motherless child. When she returns to Tockley to arrange her great-aunt's funeral ·she finds records telling her about the past of Ollerenshaw. This scene is the same as in *Jerusalem the Golden* where Clara Mangham returns to Northam to visit her mother in the hospital and she discovers notebooks and photographs which gives her the satisfaction of her true descent.

Frances too discovers many things like her mother was a cheerful person who had a lover. She identifies with her mother a lover who is married. Frances thinks of Karel and surprisingly her conflicts calm down because she feels curiously at home and like Clara the satisfaction of her true decent.

So far the conflict of the woman characters in Drabble's novels has been on the personal level but in her recent novels she handles global problems, like fighting against evil and hence the conflict is less because by now the women are emancipated to considerable extent. *The Radiant Way* and *A Natural Curiosity* are the persistence of evil in the world. The protagonists here are three women representing three intellectual disciplines. Liz represents Medical Science and Psychiatry, Alex English Literature and Esther Art History.

Liz is discovered and her problem begins when her second husband Charles is going to divorce her and marry Henrietta for whose family Liz's mother has worked as a domestic servant. Liz is jealous of Henrietta and decides to remain single and not to marry because life, without sex and its complications is easier. However, the conflict in her mind continues because she is upset about the fact that she as a psychiatrist is not able to understand her own problems. Is she efficient as a therapist? She has doubts about her own self:

> I am as serviceable as I ever was. But how can I be, when I know that I do not understand my own problems, when I know that I do not know, when I have been obliged to admit that I do not stand on solid ground, when my patterns are obscure to me?
>
> The wounded healer. But that is another concept: that is the concept of the healer whose knowledge of the malady springs from a fellow sickness, from a diagnosed fellow sickness.
>
> Is there perhaps an analogy with the faithless priest? Liz, a child of the North of England and daughter of an irreligious house, does not know much about Catholicism, but has read her Graham Green and dimly recalls the nation that even the unworthy vessel, can minister the true sacrament. Her rational self accepts this as rational: it is the nature of the healing, not the spirit of the healer, that is of value both to rational and religious man.

She decides that she has "a spiritual body odur." She has deceived her own training analyst by denying any memories before 4 years old. But we learn that Liz has suppressed the memory. It is revealed to the readers when she returns to Northam to sort out her dead mother's belongings.

Alex the leading character in the sequel *A Natural Curiosity* faces conflicts right from her childhood because her parents are liberals. Her marriage too is filled with conflicts because she falls madly in love with her baby son and rejects her unsatisfactory husband. He conveniently drowns himself and Alex marries a socialist school teacher who has published a novel but fails to progress further. Alex is disillusioned and eventually falls in love with Brian's friend, Otto. However, Otto goes to Washington to teach and Alex suffers in silence. Here we see the complications in the sex life of emancipated women. Although the woman of today is emancipated, the feminine sensibility does not allow her to express freely and so woman like Alex suffer in silence.

The third protagonist, Esther, the art historian faces the same conflict as Rosamund Staccy of *The Waterfall*. She cannot have a normal love relationship and all her relationships have consisted of an effort to avoid normal sexual intercourse. Esther thinks that all those who have normal sex life are very very sick people. She also talks obsessively about her potted palm, as if it were a pet, presumably to hide her real emotions or lack of them. She has chosen a platonic love in an effort to avoid 'normal sexual intercourse.' Here one finds Esther to be a sick person and fighting a sex conflict within herself. There is nothing wrong with normal sex relationship. Esther does not understand this and avoids normal sex relationship.

The novel-sequence ends with the three women friends going on an holiday to Italy and Brian finding inspiration to write another novel. We find that in her later novels, there is a sharp change in focus from the particular to the general. Earlier, we find that the conflict of the women characters was personal. They were issues which were concerned with relationships to parents, children, husbands and lovers. In *A Summer Bird Cage, The Garrick Year* and *The Millstone* we see young woman characters faced with the conflict of entering adulthood, whether to enter adulthood and accept sex or to remain aloof and avoid being an adult.

When Drabble was asked in an interview whether she was working out her own problem in her first three novels, Drabble answered evasively:

> It's almost inevitable, I think, that one should write about ones own age group and the preoccupations of it.[8]

In her later novels, it is observed that like the author the characters experience a mid-life reappraisal of self. The old values, ways and ideas no longer hold, but the new way is not yet clear. They are obsessed less with their past than with the quality and significance of the lives they are now leading—lives which strikingly resemble those of their associates. Initially, conflicts in the minds of characters were created by tensions in career and about the meaning of life but gradually, Drabble started writing about themes larger than the self.

The Ice Age depicts individual characters and the nation in the grip of crisis of various kinds—imprisoned, frozen into frustrating inaction. In *The Middle Ground* little seems to be happening and the characters suffer from monotonous existence. And what is happening to individuals clearly reflects in turn, to what is happening to the British society as a whole.

Fox Genovese claims: "it is hard to avoid the suspicion that Drabble is speaking in two languages at once—that of a female being on the one hand, that of first class Cambride graduate on the other."[9]

Fox Genovese is right when she says this because the conflict of the woman characters of Drabble's novels is between 'female self-consciousness' and 'artistic self-consciousness.'

Margaret Drabble is able to portray this with great depth and considerable subtlety because she is a writer with an acute feminine sensibility.

REFERENCES

1. de Beauvoir. *The Second Sex* tran. H.M. Parshley (New York: Alfred A. Knopf, 1953) 306.

2. Hilde Bruch. *Eating Disorders: Obesity, Anorexia Nervosa and the Person Within* (New York: Basic Books, 1973) 207.
3. Susan Spitzer. "Fantasy and Femaleness in Margaret Drabble's *The Millstone Novel*," 11 (Spring 1976) 227-45.
4. Nancy S. Hardin. "An Interview with Margaret Drabble," *Contemporary Literature*, 14 (Summer 1973) 273-95.
5. Mary Dary. *Beyond God the Father: Towards a Philosophy of Women's Liberation* (Boston: Bacon Press, 1973) 29.
6. J.C. Cooper. *An Illustrated Encyclopaedia of Traditional Symbols* (London: Thames and Hudson, 1978).
7. M.V. Libby. "Fate and Feminism in the Novels of Margaret Drabble," *Contemporary Literature*, 16, 2 (1976) 91.
8. Peter Firchow ed., "Margaret Drabble in the Writer's Place," *Interviews on the Literacy Situation in Contemporary Britain* (Minneapolis: University of Minnesota Press, 1974) 121.
9. Elizabeth G. Fox. "The Ambiguities of Female Identity: A Reading of the Novels of Margaret Drabble," *Partisan Review*, 46, 2 (1979) 234-48.

5

Ma Drabble: Drabble as a Novelist of Maternity

Margaret Drabble has for years lived in a comfortable house at Hampstead with her children. While she has made some very skeptical comments about marriage, she is very positive about motherhood. In an interview with Diana Cooper Clark she says:

> I see motherhood in such positive terms that I feel almost embarrassed to state it. I think it's the greatest joy in the world. But it is also a very personal thing. I just happen to like it.[1]

Drabble has portrayed the mother-child bond in many of her novels, and this has earned her the title 'novelist of maternity' and have drawn female readers empathetically to her work. Also subjects like child-rearing, etc., are discussed in her work in great detail.

In *The Millstone* Rosamund's first experience of a maternity clinic comes as a shock. She does not expect to have to wait but soon becomes adept at slipping her card into the pile so as to be called on earlier. It is a shock to her to be examined by five medical students, one after another. Eventually she is drawn into the conversation with the other pregnant women. She talks to them and feels one with them in spite of being outcast because of her unmarried status and high education. Rosamund explains that at the end of six months the 'pull of the nature' was so strong that "I felt more in common with the ladies of the clinic than with my own acquaintances."

Thus, through Rosamund Drabble shows that pregnancy brings an awareness of the facts and feelings of maternity very remote from scholarly life. Also, it arouses a feeling of affinity and oneness with other women, though different in status.

In *The Millstone* Drabble effectively shows the involvement of the mother with the child. Rosamund, the heroine, suddenly discovers that her daughter has a dangerous heart defect and has to undergo a risky operation, Rosamund is shown restlessly shifting on her bed, unable to sleep. She is full of agony and worry for the child. This state of Rosamund's mind reveals the fact that however high education a woman may have taken—for here Rosamund is doing her Ph.D.—however successful she may be academically, yet once when she becomes a mother, the maternal instincts are the strongest. Margaret Drabble, obviously, is concerned with the maternal instincts which cannot be suppressed by formal education. She shows, through the character of Rosamund that motherhood, to a woman, is a basic instinct which over rationality is associated with education.

Another situation that Drabble describes in the same novel is when Rosamund is not allowed to see the child for two weeks after the operation. She becomes desperate and restless. All her efforts to remain calm and polite fail. It is the maternal instinct that comes above all and she starts shouting in a hysterical manner: "I don't care about anyone, I don't care, I don't care, I don't care" (*M.*, 133).

After she becomes a mother all her former reserve, intellectuality and dislike for fuss are kept aside. The only thing that seems to matter to her is the precedence of the child. This incident in the novel shows Drabble's tremendous capacity to write about motherhood. The interaction between the mother and the child is for Drabble the most beautiful relationship in the world. For Drabble's heroine "a room of one's own" is usually a place to have a baby but it is, at the same time, a testing ground for knowledge and wisdom because Drabble's heroines are intellectual, educated women who want to have a career but, at the same time, combined with marriage and children. Therefore, it can be said about Drabble's heroines that they resent pregnancies but are overwhelmed with love when the children are born.

Rosamund in *The Millstone* realises that she is pregnant while she is at work on her thesis in the British Museum's Reading Room and the images of Elizabethan Sonnets are abruptly blotted out by those illegitimate pregnancies:

> gin, psychiatrist, hospitals, accidents, village maidens drowned in duck ponds, tears, pain, humiliations. Nothing at that stage resembling a baby (*M.*, 34).

She tries to have an abortion with alcohol and hot baths but the attempts are unsuccessful. It is only then that she realises that the baby is going to be real and she starts facing the realities of life. In the doctor's waiting-room she finds among her fellow patients, "representatives of population whose existence I had hardly noticed" (37). Rosamund is drawn into the dreary realm of the expectant mother's story swapping at the clinic:

> The degrading truth was that there was no fascination to us in that condition, and indeed few topics anywhere, it seems. Birth pains, fear and hope, these were the subjects that drew us together in gloomy care, and so strong was the bond that even I, doubly, trebly outcast by my unmarried status, my education and my class, even I was drawn in from time to time and compelled to prefer some anecdote of my own (*M.*, 60).

Thus, Drabble's Rosamund discovers community by giving birth. Drabble wrote this novel while she was expecting her third baby. In an introduction to a school edition, Drabble clarifies:

> I wrote it while I was expecting my third baby.... In some ways I wrote...to cheer myself up...and trying to resolve the problem of my something that it is so disagreeable and humiliating and at times painful and frightening should also be so important and rewarding.[2]

Drabble considers Rosamund's single state unimportant and declares that she wanted to write about the experience of maternity, 'the amazing delight I felt in my first baby.' In this chapter Drabble wrote this in an introduction to a school edition. Unfortunately, the school girls took it in the other way round and thought it very courageous to have babies while still unmarried. Drabble was alarmed to find this. For Rosamund it was possible because she had the use of her parents' flat and enough money to pay for help while she goes to the British Museum Library to carry on her research work, whereas the school girls were totally dependents. In fact, Margaret did not want to give any such message, and was shocked to learn the adverse effect of her writing.

It is commonly said that life for a woman is never complete without children. This is a Victorian view. Though Drabble is a contemporary novelist, many of her views are Victorian. She has said that she would rather be at the end of a dying tradition than at the beginning of an unknown one. So, children in Margaret Drabble's novels play an important part. They are not important or main characters but she skilfully uses them at decisive moments of action. For example, Rose Vassiliou is taught by her governess, from the time she is a child that wealth and excessive money is not good. Having or keeping too much of money was sin *and so* Rose *when* she sees a newspaper photograph of an African child as the victim of a civil war, sitting naked besides its mother's corpse: "its face lost, its eyes sagging blank with nothingness" (*N.E.*, 115), gives away a big part of her money to help the victims. The picture of the child creates in her a feeling of pity and love and arouses the maternal instincts so that she voluntarily gives up all her inherited wealth.

In the same novel, *The Needle's Eye,* Margaret Drabble describes a very touching scene between a mother and the child. A deformed boy and his mother bidding goodbye outside a hospital:

> and she had kissed him so tenderly, and he had run off, waving, smiling, radiant, illumined, his mother waving with a tender pride... (*N.E.*, 246).

Similar examples can be found in almost all her novels: Alison Murray's daughters in *The Ice Age*. One hopelessly retarded by cerebral palsy and the other a sullen and jealous adolescent, tearing their mother into two by their conflicting demands on her emotions. Jane Gray's son in *The Waterfall* howling with misery day after day as she leaves him for his own good, at nursery school.

In the lives of Drabble's heroines, children are a stabilising force. The young women are tempted into extramarital or adulterous affair yet they cannot bear to be separated from their children. In *The Waterfall*, Jane's husband, Malcolm, does make an isolated attempt to exert a claim on the children but Jane's strong maternal instincts do not allow it and he steps back quickly. He plays the role of a cuckolded and outraged husband from romance stories much more than a model of family concerns. But Christopher Vasiliou, Rose's husband in *The Needle's Eye* is a different case. He sends a telegram to Rose stating that he is leaving England with children, he has in his possession for the purpose of taking them to the Bryanston estate in Norfolk which was the maternal house of Rose.

Rose becomes desperate as a mother. She just cannot live without her children. She has a lover, she has her life but as a woman children are very important to her and after much legal wrangling she chases after Christopher. He has set a trap, perhaps knowingly, by having the *rescue scene arranged* at Rose's home. Rose wants to disengage herself totally from Christopher. He realises this and is aware that he would never be able to win the children back through a legal suit. So he attempts a melodramatic manoeuvre that shock Rose into seeing things more his way. She becomes furious at Christopher's way of getting the children's custody but decides to sacrifice herself for the sake of the children.

Motherhood in Drabble's novels is a form of redeeming love, a sacrifice of blood and suffering. Rose makes a sacrifice of her life for the sake of her children and decides to take back Christopher. This form of self-sacrifice is a heroic gesture by Rose. As a child she had imagined herself to be reincarnation of Christ and she sacrifices herself for her children, for humanity. The association of the child Rose, motherhood and the incarnation is supported by the image of Simone's own sacrificing 'pelican like' mother who had fed her with own blood. The pelican tearing its breast to its young. On the literal level also every mother nourishes her embryo with her blood.

Every mother in her divine power of bringing forth new life, has something in her of the creator, and women as mothers are specially privileged. Drabble imagines and writes about things which are away from the modern scientific world but as said earlier she preferred the old tradition. So Rose's motherhood is to be read as a creativity and sacrifice. She reconciles flesh with spirit. The Emma in *Garrick Year* feels extreme joy in the company of her daughters. She realises that her unhappy marriage is not at all important to her when her daughter just narrowly escapes from being drowned in the river. The drowning incident brings the husband and the wife close and the family goes out on a picnic. Emma calls it an harmonious outing in the country. She and David manage to lie among the greenery that afternoon. But just when the children are so happy and the family is relaxed, she sees a snake grabbing the beautiful wheep which they all had admired. She is shocked and horrified. But she keeps quite and pretends to be enjoying, again, for the sake of children:

> But 'Oh well, so what,' is all one can say, the garden of Eden was crawling with them too, and David and I had managed to lie amongst them for one whole pleasant afternoon. One just has to keep on and to pretend, for the sake of the children not to notice. Otherwise one might just as well stay at home (*G.Y.*, 172).

In an interview with Barbara Milton, Margaret Drabble, says clearly that a woman makes great sacrifices for her children and is an unselfish love:

> I certainly feel the mother child relationship is a great salvation and is an image of unselfish love, which is very hard to get in an adult relationship, I think, if not impossible.[3]

Pregnancy is a way of knowing, a process of education that not only helps Rosamund work 'with great concentration and clarity' on her thesis, but also makes real to her the abstractions of the human condition:

> I had always felt for others in theory and pitied the blows of fate and circumstance under which they suffered but

> now, myself, no longer free, myself suffering, I may say that I felt it in my heart (*M.*, 68).

In an interview with Dee Preussner Margaret Drabble says:

> Having children gives you an access to an enormous common store of otherness about other people. This is how I learned that other people really existed.[4]

Drabble claims that a positive model for mothering was Mrs. Swift, her mother-in-law, who created a demonstrably loving family home which contrasted so strikingly with her own inhibited one. Her relationship with her mother was a complicated one because her mother felt very insecure and depressed because of 'class reasons.' She spoke *broad yorkshire* and was the opposite of charming. She was aggressive, rude, difficult, shy, all in one which meant that their social life was terribly difficult.

In England, social life is given a lot of importance and most of the deep scars resulted from social encounters. Margaret Drabble felt that there was no way you could have friends and that made her very insecure. Drabble says:

> My mother ground her teeth and every body said, 'How unattractive.'[5]

This 'grinding of teeth' had a painful effect upon the family and had an effect on her fiction as well. Throughout her life she has looked for 'mother figures' and established 'imitative' relationship with other women—the first model for which was her relationship with her older sister Antonia Susan, whom she used to tag round after when they were children. This sister is A.S. Byatt, the noted novelist and critic, and for some time senior lecturer in English and American Literature at University College, London.

It is perhaps because of these reasons that Drabble writes so explicitly about motherhood. Furthermore, subjects of child rearing are also described as beautiful experience in her novel. Her heroine thinks it as a very sensual pleasure (Rosamund in *The Millstone*).

Rosamund was basically a very orthodox person who feared sex. In fact, it is love that she fears and she is that type of person who wants "touch without contact" (*M.*, 28). She does not like to get involved with people and be close to them. But during her pregnancy, Rosamund has inklings that becoming a mother will necessarily involve her with other human beings. However, she makes pregnancy as an excuse to keep away from social contacts and works for more number of hours on her thesis. She does not believe that just because of one baby she should ruin her career. Nancy Hardin has described Rosamund as "a competent and self-reliant young scholar." But Marion Vlastos Libby has found Rosamund's accomplishments as 'rather chilling.'

Motherhood brings a real change in Rosamund. However, she does not make a mess of mothering like Emma. She quickly gives up breast feeding because "she grew frantic at the way her clothes got covered with milk" (*M.*, 96) although the whole thing gave her profound pleasure. This is an obvious example of Drabble's tremendous capacity to write about motherhood. Further, the same heroine of Drabble describes sexual pleasure in giving birth. In the final labour she feels "sensations which though unbelievably violent were now no longer painful but indeed almost a promise of pleasure" (*M.*, 85).

After she delivers, she lies awake, resisting the sleeping pills she has been given, 'unable to get over her happiness.' Rosamund, obviously, speaks for her creator:

> I was not much used to feeling happiness: satisfaction, perhaps, or triumph and at times excitement and exhilaration. But happiness was something I had not gone in for a longtime, and it was very nice (*M.*, 87).

Of course, being a mother is great happiness and a great achievement and becoming a mother was a significant development in Rosamund's life. It would affect her relationship with all the people in general.

Pregnancy, giving birth, love for the baby, anxiety, etc. are some aspects of motherhood which Drabble writes about but in the *The Realms of Gold* she writes about motherhood from a very different angle.

Adrienne Rich thinks that daughters naturally turn to their mothers for "mutual confirmation from and with another women."[6] But Frances, the heroine of *The Realms of Gold* and her sister Alice do not receive this confirmation from their mother, a gynaecologist who campaigns for population control and 'more abortion, not less,' a woman who doesn't 'care much for sex' although "she likes sexual attention and demands it from the men around her" (*R.G.*, 78-79).

Frigidity and gynaecology, Frances thinks are a deadly combination which may have killed her sister who committed suicide. Frances believes in her mother's passion for population control. She would have spoken her belief aloud had she not feared that her mother would not mind it.

We find that Drabble's heroine is portrayed as a loving and kind mother deeply attached to her children but, at the same time, she quite frequently has a difficult relationship with her own mother. Frances in *The Realms of Gold* feels that her mother is a woman without real affection. She observes quite acutely:

> although in theory a feminist, speaking frequently of the need to emancipate woman from the chosen of domesticity and child rearing, (her mother) not to like other women. Not even her daughters (*R.G.* 81).

Matrophobia is the fear not of one's mother or of motherhood but of 'becoming one's mother,' and Frances spends her adolescence trying to deny that she is her mother's daughter.

She had pursued sex with determination rather than pleasure, resolving that whatever she turned out like, at least she wouldn't be like her mother. She correctly identifies lady Ollerenshaw as an unmotherly figure. This makes Frances, in effect, a motherless child and, "the woman who felt 'unmothered' may seek mothers all her life."[7]

This is what Frances finds when she returns to Tockley to arrange her great aunt's funeral. In her mother's cottage, Frances re-enacts a scene from an earlier novel by Drabble, *Jerusalem the Golden*. Both the novels are about coming home and discovering one's mother. In *Jerusalem the Golden*, Clara comes home and finds the old photographs and exercise books of her mother which prove that before marriage her mother had vitality and aspiration long since quenched. Looking at them, Clara feels kindship with her mother, feels "for the first time the satisfaction of her true descent." In *The Realms of Gold* also there is a similar scene when Frances Wingate opens Constance Ollerenshaw's desk, she too finds:

> records going back into the dim reaches of the dusty Ollerenshaw past.... Nearly as indecipherable as hieroglyphics, really as sparse in their information as Phoenician shopping lists, they contained a past, a history... (*R.G.*, 299).

What Frances discovers are pictures of her mother as a young woman, proving—as Mrs. Mangham's old photographs had to Clara "that she had been a beautiful girl." She discovers school certificates, love letters and the secret of her aunt:

> a birth certificate for a daughter born to Constance Ollerenshaw, June-15, 1914 in a nursing home in Lincoln: a death certificate for the same child, who had died eighteen months later (*R.G.*, 301).

Frances further discovers that the child's father had been married and had died young, leaving a widow and two children. Frances thought of Karel as she read of Constance because he too was married and had two children.

Curiously, Frances feels at home and in identifying with Constance, she at last finds the mother figure and, like Clara, the satisfaction of her true descent. She even feels satisfied when the lawyer Harold Barnard opens the door and comments, "You could have been Constance herself fifty years younger" (*R.G.*, 304).

Among discoveries that Frances is making is the one of a mother-figure who confirms her, who illuminates and expands her sense of actual possibilities as Adrienne Rich points out:

> The quality of the mother's life is her primary bequest to her daughter, because a woman who can believe in herself, who is a fighter, and who continues to struggle to create

> liveable space around her, is demonstrating to her daughter that these possibilities exist.[8]

In identifying with Constance Ollerenshaw, Frances does not seek to emulate the details of her life—they were tragic—but its quality which include Lost love, rejection, puerperal fever, guilt, interfering vicars, the death of a loved child, persecution by parents (*R.G.*, 302).

At the beginning of the novel, *The Realms of Gold*, Frances Wingate is an isolated person, alienated from her lover and her children, alone in an insulated, air conditioned hotel room and at the end of the novel, she is full of joy. No longer depressed or despairing because she is living with Karel and their two sets of children. She is refreshed and reoriented by the spiritual mother. Frances search for a mother returns her to her happy self.

Thus Drabble's heroine is loving, kind and a self-sacrificing one who enjoys motherhood though she herself has a very difficult relationship with her own mother as in the case of Clara in *Jerusalem the Golden* and Frances in *The Realms of Gold*.

Drabble, the mother of three children, started writing novels because of an unexpected motherhood which came her way. She started her career as an actress and even gained a reputation as a gifted one for the career, but she became pregnant earlier than intended and thought the writing profession a convenient one. However, in *The Garrick Year* she writes, the motherhood she had dreaded, "turned out to be one of my greatest joys."[9]

Drabble made the above remark in 1964 when only one of her children was born. As the other children came along and grew up she felt compelled to protect them from fictional invasions of privacy because by now she was a celebrity. Her later novel *The Middle Ground* (1980) is dedicated to her daughter, 'My darling Becky.' It's about being a mother to teenage children and knowing that the children are going to be gone any minute now and you have done all the things in your life, you meant to do for them.

Though this book clearly portrays Drabble as a novelist of feminine consciousness, it largely shows the mother's relationship with her grown up children. Kate in *The Middle Ground* has very friendly relationship with her eldest son Mark. She even talks with him about her lover who has left her for a woman in Cambridge. She finds she is pregnant and this late pregnancy worries her as she is a woman of forty. She confides in her son and he advises her to get rid of the baby and forget it.

While reading this piece of Drabble's novel one really wonders—Is such a mother son relationship possible? Can mothers talk so freely about their 'inner-life' to their son? Drabble here, has crossed *the modernist of the modern* and in the 21st century, this could be possible if more and more writers wrote like this and more film makers showed such scenes of close relationship with ones mother rather than getting angry and furiated by doubting the *purity of the mother.*

Drabble shows in her writings that being a mother to small infants is different and being a mother to teenagers are different things. Kate's children are loveable and healthy but everybody else in the book seems to have problematic children: rebels, misfits, Ted and Evelyn's son Sebastian is a punk, who is imprisoned for:

> drinking drugs, late nights, absent nights, theft.... All the tenants have their own theories about what went wrong, but most agree that it must have something to do with Ted's overbearing personality and ridiculously high expectations (*M.G.*, 80).

Ted works for the World Health Organisation and has a career which is erratic and successful at the same time having qualified as a microbiologist and as a doctor, he works on mosquitoes, monkeys and tropical diseases. He, perhaps, has the same expectations about his son, but the son falls short of the expectations of his father and goes the wrong way.

The novel is full of mad women, dead and abandoned babies, family breakdown. Evelyn visits families where children are neglected and abused and visits a Day care centre where they are cruelly treated. The narrator, through Evelyn's consciousness, tells us drily about force-feeding and harsh punishments such as being locked in a cupboard. These are fatherless children whose mothers have to work and who envy Joan, the woman in charge because she has a proper home and a proper husband to return to.

Children form a greater part of a woman's life and it is natural for her to love, care and feel *for them because they themselves are the creators of the little ones.*

Margaret Drabble, being a woman feels and experiences these things. Therefore, she is able to write about them with ease and confidence. Her own children have now grown up but she is still a mother and cares for them. Drabble is an active vice-patron of the Child Psychology Trust, an organisation set up to observe and treat disturbance in children. This shows that *mothers belong to the ranks of the caring.*

Thus Margaret Drabble is a novelist with a special capacity to write about the experience of motherhood. The aspects of maternity have been represented in literature through the centuries, but until recent years relatively few novelist themselves were mothers, and Drabble approaches the subject with first-hand experience into insights that have not been available to men writers or to childless women writers. She has said, for her personally, motherhood has been 'the greatest joy in the world' and she has a sharp awareness of the mixed delights and anxieties of parenthood. This relationship is something unique and asserts once again the Feminine Sensibility in her novels.

REFERENCES

1. Interview with Diana Cooper Clark, "Margaret Drabble, a Cautious Feminist," *Atlantic Monthly,* 246 (Nov. 1980) 74.
2. Margaret Drabble. *Author's Introduction to a School Edition of The Millstone* (London: Longman Imprint Edition, 1979) VIII.
3. Interview with Barbara Milton, "Margaret Drabble: The Art of Fiction," *Paris Review,* LXX 26, 569.
4. Dee Preussner. "Talking with Margaret Drabble," *Modern Fiction Studies,* 25 (1979-80) 575.

5. Iris Rozencwajg, Interview with Margaret Drabble. *Women's Studies,* 6 (1979) 339.
6. Adrienne Rich. *Of Women Born: Motherhood as Experience and Institution* (New York: Bantom Books, 1977) 273.
7. *Ibid,* 273.
8. *Ibid.,* 250-51.
9. Interview with Diana Cooper Clark, "Margaret Drabble, a Cautious Feminist," *Atlantic Monthly,* 246 (Nov. 1980) 74.

6

CONCLUSIONS

Margaret Drabble is an ambitious writer with a deep social concern. Her novels are personal in tone—lucid, seemingly confessional, eminently readable. As illustrated in the earlier chapters, she is a writer of Feminine Sensibility. The protagonists in her novels have generally followed the course and concerns of her own life as shown in the second chapter. The protagonists are young women, leaving university, getting married, having children, getting involved in affairs, raising progressively older children and reaching mid-life. The protagonists are all intelligent Arts graduates created by an even more intelligent Arts graduate who is a writer with an acute sense of feminine sensibility.

Margaret Drabble was tremendously interested in acting. If she would have been a man, she would have chosen the stage for a career because as an undergraduate she did more acting than writing. After graduation, she joined the Royal Shakespeare Company but, at the same time, she also got married and had a baby so that she had to give up her acting career. She turned to writing. She makes this clear:

> women had never been shut off from the materials of fiction. A pencil and a piece of paper...and all human life was there.[1]

She chose to write about her own experiences as a woman which are common to all women by and large. So she soon came to be known as a women's novelist. Drabble's treatment of the subject necessarily brings out the feminine sensibility as discussed and worked out in the previous chapters.

As mentioned in the second chapter, Drabble was greatly influenced by de Beauvoir's *The Second Sex*. *The Second Sex* is an anatomy of what Drabble has called "The situation of being a woman" in a man's world. It asserts that "one is not born, but rather becomes a woman."[2]

de Beauvoir describes, "How woman undergoes her apprenticeship, how she experiences her situation, in what kind of universe she is confined, what modes of escape are vouchsafed her" (*T.S.S.*, xxix).

The crucial discovery a woman makes during her apprenticeship to life is that, she is confined to a sphere created and ordained for her by men. Drabble's early novels resound with this discovery:

> in my early novels I wrote about the situation of being a woman—being stuck with a baby, or having an illegitimate baby, or being stuck with a marriage where you couldn't have a job.[3]

This has been clearly portrayed in *The Garrick Year* where the protagonist Emma wants to be the first woman news reader but she is stuck to the house because of the baby and so cannot fulfil her ambition. After marriage, she struggles for an identity of her own and does not like the mess of the union and is apalled by the filthy mess of pregnancy and birth. Drabble writes about the condition of Emma so vividly as though she herself was going through the experience. Writing so vividly about what a woman feels when she is stuck up with husband, home and family naturally reveals the feminine sensibility which is an ingredient of the feminine experience.

The Millstone, the next novel, marks the growth of Drabble's feminist consciousness. Rosamund is not a feminist heroine. She does not define herself in relation to non-patriarchal values. Like a father she is successful because she puts mind over matter. For example, when it is confirmed that she is pregnant, she does not sympathise with herself but puts mind over matter and continues with her research work at the library believing that pregnancy could not make any difference to her career. But like the other women she is a divided self.

When Rosamund becomes pregnant, she does not give up her work but continues to find satisfaction in her work even in that state. She sees no reason why her work on thesis, her proposed career of the assistant lecturership, lecturership and so on should be interrupted by having a baby. "I simply did not believe that the handicap of one small illegitimate baby would make a scrap of difference to my career" (*M.*, 94).

She says and apparently she is right because by the end of the novel, her thesis has been published and she has been offered a post at one of the most prestigious universities. This shows that Rosamund Staccy is basically a competent and self-reliant young scholar who puts mind over matter. But she is a woman and how can she avoid the functions of a woman?

When Rosamud becomes pregnant and gives birth to a child, Drabble has described at length and in detail, the process of childbirth—the pains of labour and the ultimate happiness. Further, Drabble writes about Rosamund's experience of motherhood how she gets frantic at the way her clothes get covered with milk. On the whole, it gives her pleasure but she does not like the mess of mothering and quickly gives up breast feeding. So far no writer had written about such experience of woman so vividly. Drabble writes this with first-hand experience, thus once again her feminine sensibility asserting itself throughout the novel.

The Waterfall describes a similar experience. The first fifty pages of the novel are a dramatic narration of Jane's confinement and delivery and of her growth and consummation of her passion for James. Drabble vividly describes how Jane delivers a child in a room made warm and damp by the electric heaters brought by the mid-wife from other rooms. Drabble also describes how Jane is lying on her bed, which is 'Warm and Sodden,' with blood and sweat as she has just given birth. Jane feels very peaceful in the same room afterwards when the heat and warmth of the room awaken Jane sexually and Drabble describes at length Jane's sexual encounter with James and how she experiences her first orgasm.

In a sense, one can say that Jane Gray walks willingly to the predestined path and gets wet with 'milk and blood and tears' and as Drabble writes, gets ready for the total fulfilment as a woman.

In *The Waterfall,* Drabble writes about various female experiences. In an interview with Peter Firchow, Margaret Drabble calls *The Waterfall* as the most female of her novels. To be able to write adequately about female experiences reveals the feminine sensibility of the writer.

In the same novel, Drabble has written a postscript. The postscript is a triumph of the feminine form. It reads as follows:

> No, I can't leave it without a postscript, without formulating that final, indelicate irony. I had at one point thought of the idea of ending the narrative not so much with James's death as with his impotence: the little twentieth century death. (I feel ashamed, now to have had so vicious a notion.) But, in fact, had that accident, I would quite possibly have died myself of thrombosis: since Bianca's birth I had been taking the relevant pills and probably would have gone on taking them until they killed me, which they might have well done; preferring the present to the future, however dangerously. I think I mentioned that on the eve of our departure to Norway I lay awake imagining a pain in my leg: well it was a real pain, it was swelling, a thrombic clot. The price that modern women must pay for love. In the past, in old novels, the price of love was death, a price which virtuous women paid in childbirth, and the wicked, like Nana, with the pox. Nowadays it is paid in thrombosis or neurosis: one can take one's pick. I stopped taking those pills as James lay there unconscious and motionless, but one does not escape decision easily. I am glad of this. I am glad I cannot swallow pills with immunity. I perfer to suffer, I think (*W.*, 290).

This postscript is a triumph of feminine ending because not only does its 'indelicate irony' undercut the purely fictional sublimity of Jane's affair with James, but it successfully resists its own impulse to make a final formulation. The last dramatic, heroic statement—"I prefer to Suffer"—is followed by the feminine ending "I think." Drabble has been able to achieve this kind of feminine ending only because she possesses feminine sensibility in a great deal and knows that a woman does not mind suffering for true love.

Although Drabble has made skeptical comments about marriage ("I don't know why one gets married"),[4] she has always been very positive about motherhood. In her novels, *The Garrick Year, The Millstone, The Needle's Eye* and *The Waterfall* Drabble has portrayed the mother-child bond as a strong one. Although the young heroines are tempted into extramarital or adulterous affair, they cannot bear to be separated from their children and are ready to fight with their husband as can be seen in *The Waterfall* and *The Needle's Eye.*

Children are a stabilizing force in the lives of Drabble's heroines. They are ready to make any sacrifice for the well-being of the children so much so that Rose in *The Needle's Eye* is ready to remarry Christopher for the sake of the children. Thus motherhood in Drabble's novels is a form of redeeming love, a self-sacrifice of blood and suffering which again is an attribute of feminine sensibility as can be obviously seen in the novels of Margaret Drabble.

Although the woman characters are loving mothers they are not free from conflict. In the earlier novels like *The Garrick Year* and *The Millstone,* conflicts in the minds of the women were created by tensions in career. Emma, for example, has to give up her ambition of becoming the first woman news reader on the television simply because she is married and rooted to the house on account of the children.

The other conflicts are 'self identity and sex behaviour.' Once a woman is married she remains a wife of so and so. She has no separate identity of her own. Drabble's woman is seen to be facing this conflict as discussed earlier in the book. Drabble also writes about the conflict the women protagonists face when they are growing-up from a girl into a woman. It is a very difficult stage, full of fear and doubts. Drabble has portrayed this very vividly through Sarah, Emma and Rosamund. Drabble has been successful in achieving the impact mainly because she herself is a woman who may have gone through the same situation and also because she is a writer with an acute sense of feminine sensibility.

The final section of *The Second Sex* (the book which profoundly influenced Drabble) is called *Towards Liberation*: In it de Beauvoir writes, "it is through gainful employment that woman has traversed most of the distance that separated her from the male; and nothing can guarantee her liberty in practice" (*T.S.S.*, 639). The kind of woman, Drabble imagines and writes is Jane Gray and Frances Wingate, similar to what de Beauvoir had written. But Drabble's imagination soars higher and they are independent in many other ways as already discussed in earlier chapters. But one thing can be said by creating these woman characters and by writing about female experiences, Drabble glimpses the possibility that women may free themselves from men's domination not only of their bodies and labour but of their thoughts as well.

Margaret Drabble is a contemporary writer, popular perhaps amongst the woman readers. This is but natural as she writes about their experiences. Her earlier novels are about the situation of being a woman whereas the later ones are about 'being' a woman in a man's world. Emma, Sarah and Rosamund are faced with the situation of being a woman whereas her later heroines about being a woman in a man's world. Many a time, Drabble says, she is sneered at because she is a woman writer. But at the same time, has full faith in the task she has undertaken:

> There is no point in sneering at woman writers for writing of problems of sexual behaviour, maternity gynaecology—those who feel the need to do it are actively engaged in creating a new pattern, a new blueprint. This area of personal relationship verges constantly on the political: it is not a narrow back water of introversion, it is the main current which is changing the daily quality of our lives.[5]

Margaret Drabble is right when she says this. As illustrated in the earlier chapters of the present book, her novels are about sex behaviour, maternity and gynaecology which makes her a writer of feminine sensibility.

Drabble, obviously, is the first woman writer to describe sex-experiences of women without any inhibition. She depicts with vivid impression the curiosity, pain, pleasure, satisfaction and the state of being altogether different after the act. She is a realist who avoids glorification of sex as D.H. Lawrence does through his novels. She is concerned with the 'real experience' as how it affects the feminine sensibility. Even her detailed account of the process of childbirth as in *The Millstone* and *The Waterfall* speaks of her realistic art of fiction writing. The description does resemble the naturalistic narration of the early nineteenth century novelists—Thackery, Trollop and others. But this naturalist-realist technique makes their fiction worth reading and effective. So is with Margaret Drabble, the first person narration in others reveals Drabble's naturalist-realist method. She is able to bring home her major theme as a writer of feminine sensibility.

Thus, Margaret Drabble, being concerned with the female experience as a novelist reveals the feminine sensibility through her novels. Her world is the one where women live, rejoice, suffer and learn from life. This is the world where men are welcome, but they must come with full understanding and without any pretention of being superior to women. If on the one hand, Drabble takes delight in describing woman's passionate longing for man, she is equally delighted, on the other hand, to describe the way a baby comes in this world out of its mother's womb. She is being perfectly feminine and bold enough to reveal the feminine experience. She is, without any trace of doubt, one of the major feminist writers of this century.

REFERENCES

1. Interview with Terry Colman, "A Biographer Waylaid by Novels," *Guardian*, 106 (15 April 1972) 23.
2. Simon de Beauvoir. *The Second* Sex, trans. H.M. Parshley (New York: Alfred A. Knopf, 1953) 249.
3. Interview with Nancy Poland, "Margaret Drabble: There Must be a Lot Like Me," *Midwest Quarterly*, Vol. XVI, No. 3 (Spring 1975) 225-267.
4. Nancy S. Hardin. "An Interview with Margaret Drabble," *Contemporary Literature*, 14 (Summer 1973) 277.
5. Margaret Drabble. "A Woman Writer," *Books*, 11 (Spring 1973) 4-6.

Bibliography

The following novels by Margaret Drabble are studied in detail on which is based the main argument of the book and also the conclusion finally arrived at—these novels are published by Weidenfield and Nicolson of London (unless otherwise indicated). The year of publication is given after the title:

A Summer Bird Cage, 1963

The Garrick Year, 1964

The Millstone, 1965

Jerusalem the Golden, 1967

The Waterfall, 1969

The Needle's Eye, 1972

The Realms of Gold, 1975

The Ice Age, 1977

The Middle Ground, 1980

The Radiant Way, 1987

A Natural Curiosity, 1989

Secondary Sources

Abrmas, M.H. *The Mirror and the Lamp.* University Press, 1953.

Anderson, Norman. *Christianity and World Religions: The Challenge of Pluralism.* Leicester: University Press, 1984.

Barch, Francoise. *Relative Creatures: Victorian Women in Society and the Novel.* London: Allen Lane, 1974.

Barret, Michele. *Woman's Oppression Today: Problems in Marxist Feminist Analysis.* London: Verso, 1980.

Beauvoir Simone, de. *The Second Sex.* Trans. H.M. Parshley. London: Four Square editions, 1960.

Bergonzi, Bernard. *The Situation of the Novel.* London: Macmillan, 1970.

Black, Helen C. *Notable Woman Authors of the Day.* Glasgow: David Bryce and Son, 1993.

Boulton, M.G. *On Becoming a Mother.* London: Tavistock, 1983.

Branea, Patricia. *The Silent Sisterhood: Middle-clan Woman on the Victorian Home.* London: Croom Helm, 1975.

Butler, Judith. *Gender Trouble: Feminism and the Subversion of Identity.* New York, 1989.

Cameron, Deborah. *Feminism and Linguistic Theory.* London: Macmillan, 1985.

Colby, Vineta. *Yesterday's Women: Domestic Realism in the English Novel.* Princetion: Princeton University Press, 1974.

Cooper, J.C. *An Illustrated Encyclopaedia of Traditional Symbol.* London: Thames and Hudson, 1978.

Cornillon, Susan Koppelman, ed. *Image of Women in Fiction: Feminist Perspectives.* Bowling Green Ohio: Bowling Green University Popular Press, 1972.

Courtney, William L. *The Feminine Note in Fiction.* London: Chapman and Half, 1904.

Craik, Dinah M. *A Woman's Thoughts about Women.* London: Hurst and Blackett, 1958.

Eienstein, H. *Contemporary Feminist Thought.* London: Unwin, 1984.

Ellen Cronan Rose. *The Novels of Margaret Drabble: Equivocal Figures.* Totowa, NJ: Barnes and Noble, 1980.

Ellmann, Mary. *Thinking about Women.* London: Virago, 1979.

Friedon, Betty. *The Feminine Mystique.* Harmondsworth. Penguin, 1965.

Gail, Braybon. *Women Workers in the First World War: The British Experience.* London: Croom Helm, 1981.

Gorham, Deborah. *The Victorian Girl and the Feminine Ideal.* London: Croom Helen, 1982.

Gornick, Vivian and Barbara K. Maran, eds. *Woman in Sexist Society.* New York: Basic Books, 1971.

Greer, Germaine. *The Female Eunuch.* London: Paladin Grafton Books, 1971.

Griffin, Christine. *Cultures of Feminity Romance Revisited.* Birmingham: CCCS No. 69.

Hamilton, Catherine J. *Woman Writers: Their Works and Ways.* London: Lock, Bowden and Co., 1892.

Hartman Mary S. and Lois Banner, eds. *New Perspectives on the History of Women.* New York: Harper and Row, 1974.

Heilbrun, Carolyn G. *Towards a Recognition of Androgyny: Aspects of Male and Female in Literature.* London: Gollancz, 1973.

Higden, Leon David. *Shadows of the Past in Contemporary British Fiction.* London: Macmullary, 1984.

Jacobus, Mary. *Reading Women: Essays in Feminist Criticism.* London: Methuen, 1986.

Julian, Dame. *Revelations of Divine Love.* Harmondsworth: Penguin, 1966.

Kalpan, Syeney Janet. *Feminine Consciousness in the Modern British Novel.* Urbana: Illinois Press, 1974.

Kerenji, C. *The White Goddess: A Historical Grammar of Poetic Myth,* New York.

Lawrence, M. *The Anorexic Experience.* London: The Women's Press, 1984.

Marder, Herbert. *Feminism and Art: A Study of Virginia Woolf.* Chicago: Chicago University Press, 1968.

Marwick, A. *Women at War.* London: Fontanna, 1977.

Millet, K. *Sexual Politics.* New York: Avon Books, 1970.

Minogre, Sally, ed. *Problems in Feminist Theory.* London: Routledge, 1990.

Mitchell, David. *Women on the Warpath: The Story of the Women of the First World War.* London: Jonathan Cape, 1966.

Moers, Ellen. *Literary Women.* London: The Women's Press, 1978.

Moran, Mary Hurley. *Margaret Drabble: Existing within Structures*. Corbondale, Southern Illinois University Press, 1983.

Myer, Valeri Grosvenor. *Margaret Drabble: Puritanism and Permissiveness*. London: Vision Press, 1974.

Newton, Judith L. *Women Power and Subversion, Social Strategies in British Fiction*. London: Methuen, 1981.

Nicola, Beauman. *A Very Great Profession: The Women's Novel, 1914—39*. London: Virago, 1983.

O'Neill, W.L. *The Women Movement: Feminism in the United States and England*. London: Allen and Unwin, 1969.

Rose, Ellen Cronan, ed. *Critical Essays on Margaret Drabble*. Boston, Mass: G.K. Hall, 1985.

Rosen, Andrew. *Rise Up, Women*. London: Routledge and Kegan Paul, 1974.

Rowbotham, Sheila. *Women, Resistance and Revolution*. London: Allen and Unwin, 1972.

Rowbotham, Sheila. *Women's Consciousness, Man's World*. Harmondsworth: Penguin, 1973.

Schmidh, Dorey, ed. *Margaret Drabble: Golden Realms*. Edinburgh Teras: Pan American University Press, 1980.

Sergeant, Lydia, ed. *Women and Revolution: The Unhappy Marriage of Marxism and Feminism*. London: Virago, 1982.

Sharpe, Sue. *Just Like a Girl: How Girls Learn to be Women*. Harmondsworth, Middlesex: Penguin, 1976.

Showalter, Elaine. *A Literature of Their Own*. London: Virago, 1982.

Stanley, L. and Wise S. *Breaking Out: Feminist Consciousness and Feminist Research*. London: Routledge and Kegan Paul, 1983.

Stovel, F. Nora. *Margaret Drabble: Symbolic Moralist*, Mercer Island: Starmont House, 1989.

Thomas, M.C. *Present Tendencies in Women's College and University Education*. London: Allen and Unwin, 1908.

Uglow, S. Jennifer, ed. *The Macmillan Dictionary of Women's Biography*. London: Macmillan, 1982.

Vicinus, Martha, ed. *Suffer and Be Still: Women in the Victorian Age*. London: Methuen University. Paperback, 1980.

Wandor, Michelene, ed. *The Body Politics: Writings from the Women's Liberation Movement in British*. London: Stage I, 1972.

Wearing, B. *The Ideology of Motherhood*. Sydney: Allen and Unwin, 1984.

Williams, Merryn. *Six Women Novelists*. London: Macmillan, 1987.

Zeman, Anthea. *Presumptuous Girls: Women and Their World: In the Serious Women Novel*. London: Weidenfeld, 1977.

Selected Interviews

Clare, John. "Margaret Drabble's Everyday Hell." *The Times* (27 March, 1972) 6.

Cooper-Clark, Diana. "Margaret Drabble: Cautious Feminist." *Atlantic Monthly*, 246 (November 1980) 69-75.

Creighton, Joanne V. An Interview with Margaret Drabble. In Doray Schmid, ed. *Margaret Drabble: Golden Realms*. Edinburg, Texas: Pan American University Press (1980) 18-32.

Firchow, Peter. "Margaret Drabble: The Writers Place." Interviews on The Literary Situations in Contemporary Britain, Minneapolis: University of Minnesota Press (1974) 102-21.

Hardin, Nancy S. An Interview with Margaret Drabble. *Contemporary Literature*, 14, 3 (Summer 1973) 273-95.

Kenyon, Olga. *Woman Writers Talk*. Oxford: Lennard Publishing, 1989.

Milton, Barbara. "Margaret Drabble: The Art of Fiction," LXX *Paris Review*, 20 (Fall Winter 1978) 40-65.

Parkar, Gillan and Todd, Janet. "Margaret Drabble." In Janet Todd, ed. *Woman Writers Talk*, New York: Holmes and Meier (1983) 160-78.

Poland, Nancy. "Margaret Drabble: There Must be a Lot of People Like Me." *Midwest Quarterly,* 16, 3 (Spring 1975) 255-67.

Selected Articles

Beards, Virginia K. "Margaret Drabble: Novels of a Cautious Feminist." *Critique,* 15, 1 (1973) 35-47.

Bergonzi, Bernard. "Drabble, Margaret." In James Vinson, ed. *Contemporary Novelists,* 3rd edn., New York: St Martins (1982) 184-5.

Butler, Colin. "Margaret Drabble: *The Millstone* and Wordsworth." *English Studies,* 59 (1978) 353-60.

Campbell, Jane. "Margaret Drabble and the Search for Analogy." In Jane Campbell and James Doyle, eds. *The Practical Vision: Essays in English Literature* in Honour of Flora Roy, Waterloo, Ontario: Wilfrid Laurier University Press (1978) 133-50.

Creighton, Joanne V. "The Reader and Modern and Post-modern Fiction." *College Literature,* 9 (Fall 1982) 216-30.

Davis, Cynthia A. "Unfolding Form: Narrative Approach and Theme in *The Realms of Gold." Modern Language Quarterly,* 40 (December 1979) 390-402.

"Drabble's The Middle Ground: 'Mid-Life' Narrative Strategies." *Critique,* 23, 3 (1982) 69-82.

"Feminine Endings and Beginnings: Margaret Drabble's The Waterfall." *Contemporary Literature,* 21 (Winter 1980) 81-99.

Firchow, Peter E. "Rosamund's Complaint: Margaret Drabble's *The Millstone."* In Robert K. Morris, ed. *Old Lines, New Forces: Essays on the Contemporary British Novel, 1969-1970.* Madison, NJ: Fairleigh Dickinson University Press 1976; London: Associated University Presses, 1976.

Fox-Genovese, Elizabeth. "The Ambiguities of Female Identity: A Reading of the Novels of Margaret Drabble." *Partisan Review,* 46 (1979): 234-48.

Gindin, James. "Three Recent British Novels and an American Response." *Michigan Quarterly Review,* 17 (1978) 223-46.

Harper, Michael F. "Margaret Drabble and the Resurrection of the English Novel." *Contemporary Literature,* 23, 2 (1982) 145-68.

Higdon, David Leon. *"Its Lines were the Lines of Memory Margaret Drabble, The Realms of Gold."* In shadows of the past in Contemporary British Fiction. London: Macmillan, 1985.

Joseph, Gerhard. "Antigone as Cultural Touchstone: Matthew Arnold, George Eliot, Virginia Woolf, and Margaret Drabble." PMLA, 96 (January 1981), pp. 22-35.

Korenman, Johns. "The Liberation of Margaret Drabble." *Critique,* 21 (Fall 1980) 61-72.

Lambert, Ellen Z. "Margaret Drabble and the Sense of Possibility." *University of Toronto Quarterly,* 49 (Spring 1980) 228-51.

Lay, Mary M. "Temporal Ordering in the Fiction of Margaret Drabble." *Critique,* 21 (Fall 1980) 73-84.

Levitt, Morton P. "The New Victorians: Margaret Drabble as Trollope." In Dorey Schmidt, ed. *Margaret Drabble: Golden Realms.* Edinburg, Texas: Pan American University Press, (1980) 168-77.

Libby, Marion Vlastos. "Fate and Feminism in the Novels of Margaret Drabble." *Contemporary Literature,* 16 (Spring 1975) 175-92.

MacCarthy, Fiona. "The Drabble Sisters." *The Guardian,* 13 April 1967, 8.

Mannheimer, Monica Lauritzen. "The Search for Identity in Margaret Drabble's *The Needle's Eye." Dutch Quarterly Review for Anglo-American Letters* 5, 1 (1975) 24-35.

Must be A Lot of People Like Me. Midwest Quarterly, 16, 3 (Spring 1975), pp. 255-67.

Preussner, Dee: "Talking with Margaret Drabble," *Modern Fiction Studies,* 25 (Winter 1979/80) 563-77.

"Reading Margaret Drabble's *The Waterfall.*" Ellen, Cronan Rose, ed. *Critical Essays on Margaret Drabble.* Boston: G.K. Hall, 1985.

Rose, Ellen Cronan. "Margaret Drabble's Surviving the Future." *Critique*, 15, 1 (1973) ·5-21.

Rozencwajg, Iris. Interview with Margaret Drabble. *Women's Studies*, 6 (1979) 335-47.

Sage, Lorna. "Female Fictions: Women Novelists." In Malcolm Bradbury and David Palmer, eds. *The Contemporary English Novel.* London: Edward Arnold, 1979; New York: Holmes & Meier, 1980.

Spitzer, Susan. "Fantasy and Femaleness in Margaret Drabble's *The Millstone*" *Novel*, 11 (Spring 1978) 227-45.

Stovel, Nora F. "Margaret Drabble's Golden Vision." In Ellen Cronan Rose, ed. *Margaret Drabble: Golden Realms*, Edinburg, Texas: Pan American University Press (1980) 3-17.

Whittier, Gayle. "Mistresses and Madonnas in the Novels of Margaret Drabble." *Women and Literature*, I (1980) 197-313.

Williams, Pat. "*The Sisters Drabble.*" *Sunday Times Magazine*, 6 August 1967, 12-15.

Wilson, Keith. *Jim, Jake and the Years Between: The Will to Stasis in the Contemporary British Novel.* A review of International English Literature, 13 (January 1982), pp. 55-69.